JULIA ALVAREZ

A Critical Companion

Silvio Sirias

CRITICAL COMPANIONS TO POPULAR CONTEMPORARY
WRITERS
Kathleen Gregory Klein, Series Adviser

Greenwood Press
Westport, Connecticut • London

Library of Congress Cataloging-in-Publication Data

Sirias, Silvio.
    Julia Alvarez : a critical companion / Silvio Sirias.
        p. cm.—(Critical companions to popular contemporary writers, ISSN 1082–4979)
    Includes bibliographical references and index.
    ISBN 0–313–30993–0 (alk. paper)
        1. Alvarez, Julia—Criticism and interpretation.   2. Women and literature—United
    States—History—20th century.   3. Dominican Republic—In literature.   4. Dominican
    Americans in literature.   I. Title.   II. Series.
    PS3551.L845 Z87   2001
    818'.5409—dc21   2001033482

British Library Cataloguing in Publication Data is available.

Library of Congress Catalog Card Number: 2001033482
ISBN: 0–313–30993–0
ISSN: 1082–4979

First published in 2001

Greenwood Press, 88 Post Road West, Westport, CT 06881
An imprint of Greenwood Publishing Group, Inc.
www.greenwood.com

Printed in the United States of America

The paper used in this book complies with the
Permanent Paper Standard issued by the National
Information Standards Organization (Z39.48–1984).

10 9 8 7 6 5 4 3 2 1

ADVISORY BOARD

Contents

Series Foreword

The authors who appear in the series Critical Companions to Popular Contemporary Writers are all best-selling writers. They do not simply have one successful novel, but a string of them. Fans, critics, and specialist readers eagerly anticipate their next book. For some, high cash advances and breakthrough sales figures are automatic; movie deals often follow. Some writers become household names, recognized by almost everyone.

But, their novels are read one by one. Each reader chooses to start and, more importantly, to finish a book because of what she or he finds there. The real test of a novel is in the satisfaction its readers experience. This series acknowledges the extraordinary involvement of readers and writers in creating a best-seller.

The authors included in this series were chosen by an Advisory Board composed of high school English teachers and high school and public librarians. They ranked a list of best-selling writers according to their popularity among different groups of readers. For the first series, writers in the top-ranked group who had received no book-length, academic, literary analysis (or none in at least the past ten years) were chosen. Because of this selection method, Critical Companions to Popular Contemporary Writers meets a need that is being addressed nowhere else. The success of these volumes as reported by reviewers, librarians, and teachers led to an expansion of the series mandate to include some writers with wide critical attention—Toni Morrison, John Irving, and Maya Angelou, for example—to extend the usefulness of the series.

The volumes in the series are written by scholars with particular expertise in analyzing popular fiction. These specialists add an academic focus to the popular success that these writers already enjoy.

The series is designed to appeal to a wide range of readers. The general reading public will find explanations for the appeal of these well-known writers. Fans will find biographical and fictional questions answered. Students will find literary analysis, discussions of fictional genres, carefully organized introductions to new ways of reading the novels, and bibliographies for additional research. Whether browsing through the book for pleasure or using it for an assignment, readers will find that the most recent novels of the authors are included.

Each volume begins with a biographical chapter drawing on published information, autobiographies or memoirs, prior interviews, and, in some cases, interviews given especially for this series. A chapter on literary history and genres describes how the author's work fits into a larger literary context. The following chapters analyze the writer's most important, most popular, and most recent novels in detail. Each chapter focuses on one or more novels. This approach, suggested by the Advisory Board as the most useful to student research, allows for an in-depth analysis of the writer's fiction. Close and careful readings with numerous examples show readers exactly how the novels work. These chapters are organized around three central elements: plot development (how the story line moves forward), character development (what the reader knows of the important figures), and theme (the significant ideas of the novel). Chapters may also include sections on generic conventions (how the novel is similar or different from others in its same category of science, fantasy, thriller, etc.), narrative point of view (who tells the story and how), symbols and literary language, and historical or social context. Each chapter ends with an "alternative reading" of the novel. The volume concludes with a primary and secondary bibliography, including reviews.

The alternative readings are a unique feature of this series. By demonstrating a particular way of reading each novel, they provide a clear example of how a specific perspective can reveal important aspects of the book. In the alternative reading sections, one contemporary literary theory—way of reading, such as feminist criticism, Marxism, new historicism, deconstruction, or Jungian psychological critique—is defined in brief, easily comprehensible language. That definition is then applied to the novel to highlight specific features that might go unnoticed or be understood differently in a more general reading. Each volume defines two or three specific theories, making them part of the reader's understanding of how diverse meanings may be constructed from a single novel.

Taken collectively, the volumes in the Critical Companions to Popular Contemporary Writers series provide a wide-ranging investigation of the complexities of current best-selling fiction. By treating these novels seriously as both literary works and publishing successes, the series demonstrates the potential of popular literature in contemporary culture.

Kathleen Gregory Klein
Southern Connecticut State University

Acknowledgments

I would like to acknowledge my indebtedness to the following individuals who provided vital technical assistance: Noel Ríos, Danilo Rayo, and Héctor Góngora. And, most of all, my thanks and love to Magee, who is present in every page of this work.

1

The Life of Julia Alvarez

Born on March 27, 1951, Julia Alvarez spent the first ten years of her life in the country of her birth: the Dominican Republic. On the island, she grew up in a relatively affluent environment, surrounded by a troupe of maids, whom she still remembers with genuine affection. Alvarez also experienced the security and comfort of living in an extended family. There she interacted not only with her immediate family, but with grandparents, aunts, uncles, and cousins as well. This community, with seemingly infinite options for entertainment and mischief, was not conducive to reading. In fact, during those early years Alvarez claims that she "hated books, school, anything that had to do with work" (Bing, 38). However, the culture of her homeland allowed plenty of room for creativity. Steeped in the oral tradition, Dominicans place a high value on a well-told story. The skilled storyteller is highly respected. As a young child, Julia became adroit at reciting poetry. She was often called upon to entertain guests. In fact, these early recitations impact her writing to this day. In her novels, the reader knowledgeable in Latin American literature will discover verses that belong to the Chilean Pablo Neruda, the Cuban José Martí, the Nicaraguan Rubén Darío, and, of course, to the Dominican poet, Salomé Ureña.

In spite of this seemingly blissful environment, the political climate of the Dominican Republic cast threatening clouds over the lives of the Alvarez family. The terror of living under the tyrannical rule of Rafael

Leonidas Trujillo weighed heavily on them. Moreover, Julia's father had become involved in a failed plot to overthrow the dictator. After the plot was discovered, it became only a matter to time before he would be implicated. Through the intervention of some American co-conspirators, Julia's father, a physician, was offered a fellowship to specialize in heart surgery in the United States.[1]

To the surprise of everyone in Julia's family, Trujillo's government granted Dr. Alvarez and his loved ones permission to leave the Dominican Republic. Thus, at age ten, at the gates of adolescence, Julia Alvarez was abruptly uprooted from everything that she had known and loved. "I lost almost everything: a homeland, a language, family connections, a way of understanding, a warmth," says Alvarez (Rosario-Sievert, 32). Like every immigrant family, the Alvarez's experienced considerable difficulty adjusting to the customs of their adoptive homeland. Furthermore, they arrived to the United States at a time when speaking a language other than English was considered "Un-American." Because of this, Alvarez quickly learned English, and in the process lost much of her native language. Today, she speaks Spanish with an accent, and would never consider trying to write creatively in her mother tongue.

In spite of what Alvarez lost in the move, she gained an entirely different medium of expression. According to Julia: "I say what happened to me is that we left the Dominican Republic and I landed not in the U.S., but in English," (Garza, 5). Alvarez mastered the English language, though the "losing of her accent" was not an easy task. It took significant time and effort. However, a supportive home environment allowed her to learn the new language quickly. And, as Julia repeatedly states, English became her "homeland."

There were, nevertheless, plenty of stumbling blocks along the path to Julia's assimilation into the "American Way of Life." Among them, deeply hurting the impressionable ten-year-old, were the playground taunts. Because of these taunts, Julia isolated herself from her schoolmates. However, the abuse also provided the stimulus to master English at a rapid pace. More importantly, and fortunately for her loyal readers, the trauma and the resulting isolation led her to discover books. In the realm of the printed word, Alvarez "found a portable homeland" (Rosario-Sievert, 32). Thus, at an early age, Julia Alvarez decided that she was going to become a writer. The Dominican-American knew that she had much to say, and she dreamed of one day finding a large audience.

Soon, Julia began to thrive in her adoptive homeland. Learning English at an accelerated rate—much quicker than her parents—made Julia independent from the highly restrictive traditions of the old world. And that sense of independence would soon grow even more. Middle-class Queens, New York, where the family had settled, was not considered safe by Julia's parents. Nor did they consider the local public or Catholic schools to be adequate. Thus, at age thirteen, Julia was sent off to a boarding school. From that age on, Julia never returned to live with her parents on a permanent basis. In fact, every summer, she and her sisters would be sent to the Dominican Republic with the expressed purpose of remaining in touch with their roots. During these trips, Julia began to observe the differences between cultures. She was particularly affected by the double standards between the sexes, and the significant gap in living conditions between the rich and the poor. These impressions, dating as far back as Julia's adolescence, form an integral part of her vision as a writer.

After graduating from high school in 1967, Alvarez attended Connecticut College for two years. There she won the Benjamin T. Marshall Poetry Prize. After briefly attending the Bread Loaf School of English, at Middlebury College, Julia fell in love with Vermont. She decided to transfer to Middlebury College. There she received a bachelor of arts in English, summa cum laude, in 1971. In 1973, in pursuit of her goal to become a writer, she enrolled in Syracuse University. Two years later, Julia received a master's degree in creative writing. Up until then, Julia's love was poetry; she had yet to start writing fiction in earnest. Her poems had begun to appear in print as early as 1970. Additionally, her published translations of Pablo Neruda's poetry demonstrated that she still remained connected to her Spanish-speaking heritage.

With a graduate degree in hand, Julia now had to start earning a living. In 1975, as writer-in-residence for the Kentucky Arts Commission, Alvarez traversed the back roads of that state in a small Volkswagen. In the vehicle were all her worldly possessions. Alvarez compares these two years to Walt Whitman's travels across the country. In fact, she carried a copy of *Leaves of Grass* as her guidebook (Bing, 38). The experience opened her eyes to the United States and its people. In spite of the hardships involved, Alvarez's confidence as a teacher grew appreciably. After Kentucky, she went on to a series of transitory teaching jobs in California, Delaware, North Carolina, Massachusetts, and Washington, D.C., before securing a position as an assistant professor of English at the University of Illinois in Urbana. In 1988, Julia received an offer to teach at her alma mater, Middlebury College. Ever since then she has lived in Vermont, which she now thinks of as her home state.

Throughout these years, Julia's writing career progressed, albeit very slowly. Still, her poems began appearing with increasing frequency in literary journals. In 1984, with the help of the Bread Loaf School of English director, Bob Pack, Grove Press published Alvarez's first poetic collection entitled *Homecoming*. Her verses received critical praise. In addition, her writings earned several honors. This includes, in 1987, a National Endowment for the Arts grant. Nevertheless, the large readership she had been dreaming about since childhood still eluded her. Furthermore, writing poetry seldom allows the artist to earn a living wage. Moreover, the instability surrounding Julia's life had extracted a heavy price—by the relatively young age of thirty, she was already twice divorced.

Quietly, though, without fanfare, Julia had begun to write fiction. In 1977, her stories "Father" and "The Rainfall" had appeared in print, in the *Barataria Review*. However, five more years would pass before her next work of fiction would be published. Nonetheless, Julia was increasingly encouraged by the reaction her fiction garnered in writing workshops. Although relatively early in life she had found her voice as a poet, it took years before she found her fictional voice. But as a result of Julia's persistence, the list of her published short stories began to grow steadily.

In 1986, Julia won the General Electric Foundation Award for Young Writers. Present at the awards ceremony was Susan Bergholz, one of the two people Julia credits for launching her career as a novelist. Impressed by Alvarez's reading, Bergholz approached her with the offer to become her agent. Julia accepted. The agent began to market the manuscript that would become the Dominican-American's first novel. Bergholz also served as an emotional buffer for Alvarez: she shielded the writer from the rejection letters, which didn't take long to pile up in an impressive stack. About Susan Bergholz's role in her success, Julia says "I'm very grateful to Susan as the person who really fought that battle for me, which—because of my background and because of my self-doubt—I probably would not have fought for myself" (Bing, 39).

Eventually, thanks to Susan's efforts, Julia signed a contract with Algonquin Books of Chapel Hill. Shannon Ravenel, the chief editor of this small but savvy publishing house, is the other person to whom Julia credits her success. Alvarez acknowledges that Shannon Ravenel helped form her as a writer. The Dominican-American also asserts that she will stay with Algonquin Books of Chapel Hill as long as Shannon is there, no matter how much money and perks the larger publishing houses may offer her. Shannon's "an old-time editor who does line editing and is truly interested in your growth as a writer," Alvarez says (Lyons and Oliver, 143). However, the material Julia first submitted to Shannon still required a lot of work. Over the next few years, with Shannon's help, Julia diligently revised and polished the manuscript.

In 1991, two months after Julia's forty-first birthday, *How the García Girls Lost Their Accents* was published. It was an immediate success. The public embraced the tales of the four García sisters. The critics also praised the Dominican-American's novelistic debut. Sales of the book exceeded Alvarez's wildest expectations. Her childhood dream also came true: she finally had a large audience. Furthermore, the novel earned numerous honors, including the 1991 PEN Oakland/Josephine Miles Award. In addition, it was selected a Notable Book by the American Library Association. Julia's first novel also bore one of her most notable trademarks—it drew much from the author's personal experiences. Most of the characters and incidents of *How the García Girls Lost Their Accents* were inspired by actual people and events. Like in the García family, Alvarez is one of four girls. Not surprisingly, when her debut novel appeared in print, for a few months Julia's mother refused to speak with her. The tales of the García Girls also earned the disdain of Julia's sisters. Happily, though, with the passage of time, Julia's family has become extremely proud of her and her work. In fact, she claims that many of the incidents that she invented for her first novel have now passed into the Alvarez family archives of actual events. The public has also accepted Julia's tales as its own. To date, *How the García Girls Lost Their Accents* has sold well over 250,000 copies, and that number continues to rise steadily.

Julia's personal life, like her career as a writer, began to take a turn for the better as well. After years of shifting jobs, she earned tenure at Middlebury College. In addition, and undoubtedly more important to Julia, she met and married Bill Eichner, an ophthalmologist and the father of two daughters from a previous marriage. Julia had finally set roots, and after many years of hard work, she had begun to enjoy success.

Alvarez's rapidly increasing fame also presented an unforeseen challenge. Julia now found herself at the forefront of a talented corps of Latino and Latina writers. Over the last two decades, U.S. writers of Latin American descent had finally made their voices heard. With the remarkable success of *How the García Girls Lost Their Accents*, Julia Alvarez was placed in the uncomfortable position of spokesperson, not only for her peers, but also for all Latinos and Latinas. Alvarez says "The bad part of being a 'Latina Writer' is that people want to make me into a spokesperson. There is no spokesperson! There are many realities, different shades and classes" (Fernandez, E4).

Julia's success and her unique identity posed yet another minor annoyance for her. The question many literature students ask is "Where does Julia Alvarez fit in the American literary horizon?" She is neither a Dominican in the traditional sense, nor is she thought of as a mainstream American writer. Her ethnicity places her in a distinctive position—on the hyphen of human existence, where the combinations of cultures are "strange and wonderful and painful and conflicting" (Lyons and Oliver, 141). Julia visibly recoils when, because of her ethnicity, people attempt to relegate her to the margins of American literature: "I am a Latina who writes, but not one who writes only for Latinos" (Fernandez, E4).

In fact, Julia's literary background is not restricted to a single cultural viewpoint. Alvarez is a remarkably well-read person. Furthermore, all her readings have influenced her. Therefore, when one attempts to trace her literary lineage, it spans across cultures, nationalities, and languages. She cites an endless list of authors as her favorites: Toni Morrison, Alice Munro, Louise Erdrich, Leslie Marmon Silko, Joy Kawawa, William Trevor, Annie Proulx, Karen Shields, Gabriel García Márquez, Leo Tolstoy, Dante, Sandra Cisneros, Pablo Neruda, and the list goes on and on. However, she credits Maxine Hong Kingston's *Woman Warrior* for showing her that a writer coming from outside of the mainstream can still write about the American experience. *Woman Warrior* allowed Julia to believe that there was a place in U.S. literature for her unique outlook on life.

In 1994, Algonquin Books of Chapel Hill published Julia's second novel: *In the Time of the Butterflies*. Once again it was warmly greeted by critics and the public. For this work, Alvarez selected a story that had haunted her since childhood: the lives and deaths of the Mirabal sisters—also known as *Las Mariposas*. She recalls that their deaths profoundly impacted her as a youth because "their stories ended just as ours [the Alvarez's] began" (Garza, 5). In 1986, a woman's press preparing postcards and booklets on notable Latinas asked Julia to write about the Dominican heroine of her choice. Without hesitation she chose the Mirabal sisters as her subject. It was while conducting research for this supposedly small project that Alvarez discovered the existence of Dedé, the sister who survived. *In the Time of the Butterflies* is, without question, the novel that has earned Alvarez her most devoted readers. The story of the Mirabal sisters is heartwrenching, and Julia tells it remarkably well. In comparison to her first novel, she shows considerable growth as a writer. Her second novel also earned several honors. *In the Time of the Butterflies* was named a Notable Book by the American Library Association; selected as a Book of the Month Club choice; nominated as a finalist for the National Book Critics' Award in fiction; and it was chosen one of the Best Books for Young Adults by the Young Adult Library Services Association and the American Library Association.

The events narrated in this historical novel have a strong tie to Alvarez's personal life as well. The Mirabal sisters belonged to the same political underground as Julia's father. While conducting research, Julia spent time in her former homeland interviewing those knowledgeable on the subject—in particular Dedé. The end result takes the American reader into the heart of Dominican politics during Rafael Trujillo's dictatorship via the *gringa dominicana*, an interview woman who, not unlike Alvarez, lives on the cultural hyphen. That is, she exists between cultures: the American and the Dominican, dwelling uncomfortably between them. The impact of the novel is so great, its scope so panoramic, that the rights to *In the Time of the Butterflies* have been optioned to Phoenix Pictures. The movie will be released for the Showtime channel sometime in the year 2001.

At the conclusion of the 1994–1995 academic year, Alvarez made one of the most difficult decisions of her life—she gave up her tenured position in the Department of English at Middlebury College. An associate professor, Julia loved her work as a teacher. She believes it essential to pass on the wisdom her teachers have shared with her. But Julia now wants to concentrate fully on writing, and financially she finds herself in a position to do so. Nevertheless, she has not abandoned the classroom altogether. On occasion she teaches at Middlebury, and she continues to participate in writing workshops.

In 1995, Dutton published *The Other Side/El Otro Lado*, Julia Alvarez's second collection of poetry. In these poems Julia tackles the same issues and themes that inform her novels. In fact, a somewhat novelistic style characterize her verses. The following year, Plume published a revised version of Alvarez's first poetic collection, *Homecoming*. For this edition Julia added several new sonnets that bring the number of these poetic compositions to forty-six, her age at the second printing; up from thirty-three, her age at the time the original manuscript was completed.

In 1997, Alvarez published her third novel, ¡Yo!. Again, both critics
and the public warmly received it. A sequel, of sorts, to *How the García
Girls Lost Their Accents*, the novel experiments with wresting the story
away from the storyteller who, in this instance, is Yolanda García. "This
is about the revenge of the people in a writer's life who don't usually
get to tell the story because the writer is always co-opting the experience," Alvarez says (Lyons and Oliver, 133). Once more, the novel demonstrates the Dominican-American's continued growth as a writer. The
imaginative way in which Alvarez experiments with points of view is
astonishing. As Alvarez states: "When you write a novel you have to
remember that you are telling the truth according to your characters"
(García-Tabor and Sirias, 153). Furthermore, her prose is extraordinarily
poetic. At the same time, the narrative and the multiple plots remain
crystal clear.

In 1998, Julia's collection of essays, *Something to Declare*, was published.
In these writings, Alvarez generously shares her life and her views of
the world with her readers. Fans of Julia Alvarez will be touched by the
articles' openheartedness. Those wanting to know her better are well-
served by reading *Something to Declare*. In this work Julia bares her soul
as a person, and as a writer. The nakedness of these essays invites the
derision of critics, but will deeply touch most readers.

In June 2000, Julia published her fourth novel, *In the Name of Salomé*.
Her second historical novel, it deals with the lives of two remarkable
Dominican women: the poet Salomé Ureña, and her daughter, Camila
Henríquez Ureña. In telling the women's stories, Julia also tells the story
of the men in their lives. The Henríquez Ureñas are perhaps the most
notable family in Dominican history. In October of 1997, Alvarez and
her husband traveled to Cuba to research Camila Henríquez Ureña's life
there. Alvarez's considerable storytelling abilities, as well as her pains-
taking investigation of her subjects, bring to life the volatile and passionate history of the Henríquez Ureñas. The result of her hard work
should not disappoint Alvarez's fans. Those who read the novel are destined to remember the Henríquez Ureñas' legacy.

The year 2000 has been a busy one for Julia. In September, Knopf
published her first book for children: *The Secret Footprints*. In this work,
Alvarez writes about creatures from Dominican folklore known as the
Ciguapas. These mythical beings live apart from humans, whom they
greatly fear. They come out for food only at night. The one thing that
differentiates them from us is that their feet are on backwards. This protects them from being followed to their hidden dwellings. Julia's tale
about the encounter of the two worlds constitutes a lesson on the im-

portance of leaving behind our misconceptions about those who are different from us. In October of the same year, Julia, with her husband Bill, published *The New Family Cookbook: Recipes for Nourishing Yourself and Those You Love*. Published by Chelsea Green Publishing Company, it expands on the boundaries of the cookbook genre by interspersing culinary essays among the recipes. So far, critics have praised the warmth that is conveyed in the writing. And Alvarez's busy pace continues: for in March of 2001, Knopf released her first book for young adults: *How Tía Lola Came to Stay*.

Julia Alvarez exemplifies the artist who has made great sacrifices to master her craft. Moreover, she continues to grow at her trade. Although proud of her considerable accomplishments, Alvarez is compelled to move forward, to explore new avenues in the art of storytelling. This dynamic attitude also applies to her other writings. Consequently, hard work has characterized her life. Writing is serious business for Julia Alvarez. She considers it vitally important to fully engage her readers.

Julia—like her alter ego, Yo—writes to give meaning to her life. She repeatedly claims in interviews that she writes to discover what she is thinking, to discover who she is, and to understand the world in general. More importantly, she writes as a way to reach out to others, to touch those from whom she is separated by time and distance. Like her role-model, Scheherazade (from *The Arabian Nights*), Alvarez tells stories both to save herself and to make the world a kinder, gentler place: "My heroine of all times is Scheherazade, who by the telling of stories gains her life, saves the other women in the kingdom, and transforms the sultan's hatred to love" (Lyons and Oliver, 133).

NOTE

1. I wish to clarify the use of the term "American" throughout this book. Many of Alvarez's readers are drawn to her work because of its strong political content. Currently, numerous people object to the term "American" to designate citizens of the United States. After all, America is an entire continent, and all its inhabitants, North, Central, South, and Caribbean Americans are also "Americans." However, the problem is as follows: the expression "Citizen(s) (or people) of the United States of America" proves too cumbersome to use repeatedly in writing. Therefore, this book, for the sake of avoiding repetitiveness, and with the utmost respect for all "Americans," will employ the abbreviated term to refer to people who live in the United States of America.

2

The Latino Novel

At present, Latino literature represents one of the most interesting con-
stituents of American letters. Latino and Latina writers are producing
remarkable works in every conceivable genre. Latinos, though, are far
from being an easily definable ethnic group. As a population, Americans
of Latin-American descent represent the whole spectrum of racial backgrounds. The majority of Latinos are mestizos, or people of mixed indigenous and Spanish ancestry. However, Latinos may also be black,
Asian, Arabic, Jewish, indigenous-American, white Europeans, and so
forth. What Latinos have in common is that their ancestors lived in Latin
America (and some scholars include Spain as well). With regard to language, some Latinos are fully bilingual; others are monolingual.
Therefore, what unites Latinos is neither race nor language, but culture—
a culture shaped by the heritage they share with the Spanish-speaking
nations to the south of the United States.

Although Latinos share a core heritage, their ethnic panorama is quite
complex. Many distinctions exist between them. For instance, among
Americans of Mexican descent there are strong preferences with regard
to the label they choose for identification. Some prefer the term "Chicano," which connotes an ideological alignment with the objectives of
the American Civil Rights Movement. Others reject this term, or simply
prefer the term "Mexican-American," which may or may not indicate an
individual's distance from socio-political ideals that reside in the name
Chicano.

A wide range of possible national origins divides Latinos even further. Latinos can be Puerto Rican-Americans, Cuban-Americans, Chilean-Americans, Salvadoran-Americans, and on and on. Even among these groups there are pronounced differences according to socio-economic class, religion, race, educational level, geographic region of the United States in which they reside, political leanings, etc. Thus, we see that the ethnic group that Julia Alvarez belongs to cannot be easily summed up.

With the exception of American Indians, Latinos have lived longer in the United States than any other ethnic group. Juan Ponce de León's 1513 expedition to Florida represents the first group of Europeans to set foot on what is today the U.S. mainland. Furthermore, when Pedro Menéndez de Avilés founded Saint Augustine, Florida, in 1565, he established the first permanent European settlement in North America. This enterprise took place more than half a century before the Pilgrims landed at Plymouth Rock. Both endeavors also represent the beginnings of the process of *mestizaje* in the United States—in other words, the blending of the indigenous and European races.

Latinos have been writing about their experiences in what today constitutes the United States as far back as 1542, when Alvar Núñez Cabeza de Vaca published *The Shipwrecks* in Spain. This narrative details the eight-year odyssey of the author and four other survivors of a shipwreck off the coast of Florida that claimed 400 lives. The men wandered through what today are Texas, New Mexico, and Arizona. Indigenous tribes captured Cabeza de Vaca and his men and held them in slavery. Later, through circumstances that belong in the realm of magical realism, the American Indians came to consider the Spaniards as gifted medicine men. Given their freedom, the shipwrecked crew traveled for several years throughout the American southwest before being found by Spanish slave-hunters in northern Mexico. Starting with this sixteenth century European bestseller, Latinos have never stopped writing about their lives in the United States.

In spite of the Latinos' long literary tradition in the United States, it is not until recently that their writings have begun to receive critical recognition and earn a broad readership. One of the first Latino novels to successfully enter the American literary mainstream was Rudolfo Anaya's *Bless Me, Ultima*, which appeared in print in 1972. Other notable Latino novels had been published prior to Anaya's work—in both Spanish and English—but his was the first to earn widespread acceptance. To date, more than 350,000 copies of this classic novel have been sold.

Although *Bless Me, Ultima* now enjoys an impressive readership, for decades it flourished as a cult classic. Prior to the late 1980s, well-established publishing houses were uninterested in works written by Latinos. Therefore, Latino writers depended on small publishing houses in order to see their work in print. With scant resources and poor distribution, the American reading public remained in ignorance of Latino writings. But Latino writers persisted in their efforts to break into the mainstream, convinced of the worthiness of their work. In 1983, Sandra Cisneros's *The House on Mango Street* became the first commercially successful novel written by a Mexican-American woman. Her novel opened the doors of large publishing houses for works by other Latinas.

In 1989, the Cuban-American Oscar Hijuelos, with his second novel, *The Mambo Kings Play Songs of Love*, became the first Latino—and so far the only one—to win the coveted Pulitzer Prize. The success of the Cuban-American's work sent more publishers out of their offices in search of more Latino talent. And they found plenty—especially women writers. Silenced for centuries by a patriarchal Latino culture, as well as by the historically male-dominated literary world, Latinas had much to say. And, arguably, they were saying it in a more interesting manner than their male counterparts. Although Latino writers possess considerable talent, the writings of Latinas captured the imagination of the American reading public. The established publishing houses responded vigorously to the readers' interest in Latina literature—seemingly, and unfortunately, at the expense of overlooking impressive works written by men. As a result, in the late 1980s, a group of talented Latina novelists began to emerge. The Mexican-Americans Ana Castillo, Denise Chávez, Helena María Viramontes, and Demetria Martínez are among the names that can be added to Sandra Cisneros's. The Puerto Rican-Americans Judith Ortiz-Cofer, Esmeralda Santiago, and Rosario Ferré (who had a well-established career as a writer in Spanish before switching to English) have earned the respect of readers. The Cuban-Americans Cristina García, Himilce Novas, and Achy Obejas began to experience considerable success as well. And this list is far from complete. Among these writers, Julia Alvarez represents the "other." She is the lone Dominican-American woman novelist to have achieved widespread recognition in the United States.

We need to be reminded—and it is an important reminder—that no Latino or Latina writer wants to be relegated to the margins of American literature. Most of them would assure us that they are "American" writers who happen to be Latino or Latina. When tracing the literary lineage of Latino novelists, one has to look beyond the obvious. There is neither a program, nor a Latino literary movement to which they subscribe. Moreover, Latino writers are extremely knowledgeable with regard to the American literary tradition. Like Alvarez, they cite many "mainstream" writers among their biggest influences. In essence, Latino writers, like all other writers, do not only read the works of other Latinos for inspiration—they read and draw from the entire gamut of world-renowned literature.

The experience of being a Latino or a Latina, nevertheless, does tint their work. Alvarez says that "because I am Latina, there are certain themes, concerns, ways of focusing subjects to which I gravitate" (Rosario-Sievert, 33). In fact, because of their shared heritage, many themes are common among these writers: the importance of family, the importance of religion, acculturation, cultural displacement, assimilation, politics, racism, machismo, superstition, generational differences, and so on. However, every Latino and Latina novelist asserts that he or she does not want to be read only for the content of his or her work, but also for his or her skills as a writer.

Julia Alvarez represents a highly skilled writer, regardless of her ethnicity. Two of her novels, *How the García Girls Lost Their Accents* and *¡Yo!*, for instance, defy classification. The literary critic is compelled to designate these novels as experimental. Normally, the Dominican-American's debut novel would be considered a *Bildungsroman*, or a novel that follows the development of the hero or heroine from childhood into adulthood, through a troubled quest for identity. This simple categorization is precisely what Julia Alvarez wanted to avoid when she wrote the novel. Thus, she resorts to experimentation. Inspired by Charles Baxter's novel, *First Light* (1987), Alvarez tells the story backwards. In effect, what she tries to replicate is the immigrant experience, the individual who recently arrived to a new country and is always looking back to give meaning to his or her experiences. In addition, *How the García Girls Lost Their Accents* lacks a central heroine. Instead, Alvarez makes this the story of an entire family through her experimentation with the point of view.

On the other hand, *¡Yo!* would normally be considered a *Künstlerroman*—a novel in which the central character is an artist, as in James Joyce's *A Portrait of the Artist as a Young Man*. However, again, Alvarez wanted to sidestep easy categorization of her work. Inspired by Stud Terkel's *Working* (1974), and by the writings of Walt Whitman, she strove to tell the story of the artist, but as seen through the eyes of other characters. She wanted to tell the tale from the perspective of those who have been rendered powerless to do so. And Alvarez accomplishes this admirably. Thus, once again, by means of experimentation, Alvarez's third novel eludes effortless classification.

The Dominican-American's second novel, *In the Time of the Butterflies*, should be considered a historical novel. However, as can be expected of Julia Alvarez, this categorization is not entirely satisfactory. For inspiration, like many other Latino and Latina novelists, she turns to the Latin American novel. The publication, in 1967, of Gabriel García Márquez's *One Hundred Years of Solitude*, marked the entry of the Latin American novel into literary modernity. Seemingly dormant for centuries, the Latin American novel entered the world literature scene with a resounding explosion. In fact, that period of Latin American literary production is known as "The Boom." The novels of the Colombian García Márquez and other Latin American writers became overnight bestsellers. In addition, García Márquez's work helped define a genre of modern fiction known as magical realism—which Alvarez mentions as an influence. In writings that belong to the school of magical realism, fabulous and fantastical events are included in a narrative that otherwise maintains the reliable tone of an objective realistic report. The fantastic attributes given to the characters in such novels—levitation, flight, telepathy, and telekinesis—are among the means magical realism adopts in order to encompass the often-phantasmagoric political realities of twentieth-century Latin America.

In fact, it is because of the political oppression rampant in Latin America that the novels of magical realism flourished. This artistic form of narrative allows a writer to condemn the horrors of dictatorships without becoming preachy or propagandistic. Latin American novels condemning dictatorships, however, are not a recent phenomenon. These narratives date as far back as 1838, when the Argentine Esteban Echeverría published *El matadero* (*The Slaughterhouse*), a brilliant novella that condemns the dictatorship of Juan Manuel Rosas. In 1946, Miguel Angel Asturias published *El Señor Presidente* (*The President*), an experimental novel, and a precursor of magical realism, which exposes the evils of Manuel Estrada Cabrera's dictatorship. For this effort, the Guatemalan writer won the 1967 Nobel Prize in Literature. Many other Latin American novelists have devoted considerable effort and talent to attacking dictatorships through their works. Notably among them are Augusto Roa Bastos, Mario Vargas Llosa, Isabel Allende, and Gabriel García Márquez.

It is to this rich literary tradition, then, that Julia Alvarez turns to when writing *In the Time of the Butterflies*. She reaches back into her Dominican heritage to find a horrifying tale of the abuses of Rafael Leonidas Trujillo's dictatorship. Alvarez then turns to her Latin American counterparts to learn how to tell this story. Her success is without measure. In fact, an indication of the power of her second novel is that the renowned Peruvian novelist, Mario Vargas Llosa, after reading the Spanish-language version of Alvarez's work, *En el Tiempo de las Mariposas*, was inspired to write his most recent novel, *La Fiesta del Chivo*, which also concentrates on Trujillo's dictatorship. Thus, here we have the evidence that Alvarez, like other U.S. Latino writers, is the object and subject of literary cross-pollination.

Alvarez's fourth novel, *In the Name of Salomé*, would also be considered a historical novel. This intimate yet panoramic look into the lives of Salomé Ureña and Camila Henríquez Ureña spans over two centuries of events that affect three nations: the Dominican Republic, Cuba, and the United States. This time, Alvarez experiments with the structure of the novel to escape easy classification. The stories of the two women move in opposite directions—one narrated in chronological order, the other in reverse—before they intersect in the end. As usual, the Dominican-American author challenges herself in order to provide her readers with a fresh perspective on a tale that could have easily been told in a straightforward, traditional manner. Once again, Alvarez succeeds in her experimentation. *In the Name of Salomé* represents her most bold and adventurous novel to date. Therefore, as it is easy to see, readers can always count on Julia Alvarez to test the limits of her skills as a writer.

3

How the García Girls Lost Their Accents
(1991)

In 1991, Algonquin Books, a small yet growingly influential publishing house from Chapel Hill, North Carolina, released *How the García Girls Lost Their Accents* by the Dominican-American writer, Julia Alvarez. The publication of this novel heralded the arrival of a major new talent on the American literary horizon. *How the García Girls Lost Their Accents* was warmly received by critics and the reading public. It earned as much praise for its sense of humor as for the poignancy of its interrelated stories. The ease with which the book can be read belies the time and effort Alvarez invested in learning her craft.

Initially conceived as separate stories, individual chapters of *How the García Girls Lost Their Accents* began appearing in magazines, anthologies, and journals as early as 1983, in slightly different versions from the novel. As accomplished as these stories were, however, numerous publishers rejected the manuscript of *How the García Girls Lost Their Accents* before it found a home at Algonquin Books. A less determined individual would have been discouraged from continuing in the writing profession after so many disappointments and frustrations. Thus it is fitting that after many years of hard labor, Alvarez's first work of fiction met with great success. In 1991 it won the PEN Oakland/Josephine Miles Book Award, and in 1992 the American Library Association named it a Notable Book.

How the García Girls Lost Their Accents tells the stories of the García

sisters—Carla, Sandi, Sofía, and Yolanda—and their parents, Laura and
Carlos. With Yolanda at the center of the narrative, the novel relates, in
reverse order, the sisters' brief years in their birthplace, their forced immigration to the United States to escape Dominican dictator Rafael Trujillo, their acculturation into American society, and their lives as adults.
Thus, as readers, we are taken into the fold of an immigrant family. We
get to know the Garcías intimately. We see them at their best, as well as
at their worst. We learn what their life was like on the island. We experience the terror and the pain of separation as they are obliged to leave
behind everything that was important to them. We share the family's
trauma as they learn to deal with life in their new country, the United
States. Throughout the entire process, the sisters experience the normal
pains of growing up, which are accentuated as they struggle to cope with
a new, radically different environment, different customs, and a different
language. Their loves, their losses, their triumphs, their joys, and their
sorrows are all there for us to see.

How the García Girls Lost Their Accents is a bittersweet tale characterized
by its honesty. It details what life is like in a bilingual, bicultural family.
But at the same time, it emphasizes the act of writing and the power of
language to express one's notions and feelings about the world. To bring
the reader closer into her universe, Alvarez uses Spanish words and
phrases, deliberately choosing expressions that have a marked emotional, ironic, or satirical impact. This device, overall, allows one to experience the Garcías' socio-cultural dualism and the richness of their
heritage. Although we may not share the same cultural background, we
easily come to identify with them. In the end, the reader is left with a
yearning to know more about the Garcías. Luckily, Alvarez doesn't disappoint us, and her third novel, *¡Yo!*, provides us with a family update.

PLOT DEVELOPMENT AND STRUCTURE

The reader who desires a neat, linear plot will be challenged by the
structure of *How the García Girls Lost Their Accents*. Simply defined, a plot
consists of the plan, design, scheme, or patterns in a work of fiction.
Important to the plot is the organization of incident and character in
such a way as to induce curiosity and suspense in the reader. A well-
constructed plot has an underlying structure that promises the reader
that the author is in control, and that any event she is telling will eventually make sense. Every event the writer narrates should lead to the

next logical event, and this should ultimately lead to a satisfying climax in which all of the reader's questions are answered. Although each chapter in Alvarez's novel stands alone as a story in itself, the reader might become impatient with the work's lack of unity, with its disregard for a traditional, linear, and easily discernible plot.

Since *How the García Girls Lost Their Accents* is an experimental novel, the reader may become frustrated as well with the novel's structure. The structure of a novel can be defined as the sum of the relationships of the parts to each other. The formal structure of a novel consists of its parts, chapters, and their interdependent balance. Alvarez's novel moves unconventionally: it goes backwards in time. The work consists of fifteen chapters without a linear, unifying story. The chapters are episodic, with little apparent connection to one another other than the recurring characters and themes. This makes it difficult for the reader to discern a singular storyline. The episodic nature of the novel violates the Aristotelian notion of the well-knit plot. The chapters seem to succeed one another without a probable or necessary sequence. However, the patient and persistent reader will find himself or herself rewarded with a moving tale of a family that prevails throughout considerable traumas, remaining loyal and loving to one another. They remain so in spite of being suddenly uprooted from everything that has ever been familiar and placed in a country where the language and culture are alien.

The novel is divided into three parts: Part I 1989–1972, Part II 1970–1960, and Part III 1960–1956. As these divisions indicate, the story moves from the closest point in the present of the narrative to the furthest. Part I is centered around the adult lives of the García sisters; Part II deals with their immigration to the United States and their adolescence; and Part III recollects their early childhood on the island. Each section represents a major change in the lives of the family, and each chapter narrates a rite of passage that a character, or several characters, undergoes.

Part III, the novel's last section, begins with the chapter titled "The Blood of the Conquistadores." From a structural standpoint, the ending of this chapter provides the novel's most intriguing moment. As will be discussed in the section on "Point of View," the rapidly changing vantage point throughout this chapter reflects the utter chaos of the García's last hours in their homeland. The chapter closes with Chucha's point of view, told in the first-person. Chucha, the Haitian maid, remains alone in the house after the family's departure. A practitioner of the voodoo religion, Chucha's spiritual powers are such that the other maids fear her. In the chapter's concluding segment, Chucha becomes the medium through which the García sisters are able to access their island past; a past they barely remember because of the young age at which they left. Chucha, then, becomes the gateway through which the sisters can retrieve the stories of their childhood years on the island. The literary device of the medium as the key to retrieving the voices not only of the dead, but also of what would constitute the forgotten past, is one that we will see Alvarez employ in her other novels. In this case, Chucha acts as the agent who unlocks the sisters' subconscious. Through her ability to access the voices of the past, she allows the sisters to recover memories that because of their young age would have remained forgotten. This allows us, then, to move backwards in space and time, in a believable manner, to the family's homeland via the earliest memories of the García sisters.

The last chapter, "The Drum," is replete with thematic metaphors as well as clues to unravel the novel's structure. For instance, in this chapter, although told in the first-person, Yolanda is not yet able to communicate effectively in the adult world because of her young age. Thus, she communicates through her drum. The chapter revolves around a toy drum that Yolanda receives as a gift and a recently born kitten that she steals away from its mother. Although being warned that taking the kitten from the safety of its mother would violate its natural rights, Yolanda still does so. As she walks away from the shed where the mother lives with her litter, she hears the adult cat calling and she flees in panic. At first she hides the kitten in the hollow of her drum, but as the kitten responds to the mother's call, and the mother begins moving in the direction of the cry, Yolanda panics further, flinging the kitten deep into the garden bushes. Yolanda suffers afterwards from guilt. She can't sleep in peace; she sees the mother's shadow in her room at night. As a metaphor, the kitten represents the García girls, who cannot find adequate protection in the hollow confines of their homeland. They, like the kitten, are flung out at a very tender age into a harsh world. They have been forcefully removed from the safety of their nest. The memory of this terrifying incident, with the subsequent guilt, stand as the metaphor for the motivation behind the stories that Yolanda must tell in order to exorcise her demons, in order to come to terms with her dual and bewildering identity. She thus becomes an artist in order to understand the trajectory of her life. At the end of this chapter the entire structure implodes. The reader is situated both at the beginning and at the end of the story. Past and present merge into one as Yolanda reveals herself as the narrator and architect of the entire saga of the García sisters. With this breakdown in the structure of the narrative, like a collapsing house of cards, Alvarez brings her first novel to a close.

POINT OF VIEW

One of the most interesting aspects of Julia Alvarez's writing style is how she employs the point of view. Simply defined, the point of view is the position of the narrator in relation to his or her story. In other words, it is the outlook from which events are related. There are many variations and combinations of points of view, but three basic forms can be distinguished. First we have the omniscient, third-person narrative. In using this point of view, the author moves from character to character, place to place, and episode to episode with complete freedom, giving herself access to the thoughts and feelings of her characters. Omniscient means "all-knowing." This is probably the most commonly used point of view and it is one that has been established in the novel from its inception. Such a point of view, however, does not require the author to stay outside of her narrative. She is still free to interpolate her own commentaries and to provide the reader with whatever information she deems appropriate at a time of her choosing. Second in this discussion of points of view is the third-person limited. Here the author chooses a character and the story is related in such a way that the field of vision is confined to him or her alone. This viewpoint differs from the omniscient narrator in that it has a limited point of view; the narration is confined to what that character knows about events. It is told by an invisible narrator that uses the pronouns "he" or "she" when telling that character's story. Finally there is the first-person point of view. From this vantage point the story is told by one of the characters in the first-person, using his or her own voice. It differs from the third-person point of view in that the first person tells the tale using the pronoun "I."

The choice that an author makes regarding the point of view is an important one. Basically, the writer selects the point of view that she deems best suited for the story she has to tell. A first-person narrator, for instance, places the reader in the midst of the action, thus she or he participates vicariously in all the events. The reader will share the innermost thoughts, feelings, and attitudes of the protagonist with a sense of recognition and identity. The first-person voice enables the narrator to speak with conviction, and this gives realism, or verisimilitude, to the story. But unlike the omniscient, or all-knowing narrator, the powers of the author are restricted. The descriptive freedoms of the author are confined to the viewpoint of the one character. On the other hand, a third-person narrator, such as the third-person omniscient and the third-person limited, places the reader at a distance from the story. Because of this, the reader loses the conviction and the intimacy that he or she finds in the first-person narrative. It does, however, allow the author a greater degree of freedom from which she can employ a more authoritative voice. It allows her to describe actions and to explain their meanings in more detail.

In *How the García Girls Lost Their Accents*, Alvarez opts for all three points of view: the third-person omniscient, the third-person limited, and the first-person. Her switches in viewpoint can, at times, confuse the reader. Alvarez, however, helps the reader somewhat by providing a subheading after each chapter title, and also by listing the name of the character, or characters, on which the narrative is concentrating on the upper right-hand corner of the odd-numbered pages. Usually this is the character from whose vantage point the story is told. For instance, the first chapter, titled, "Antojos," is followed by the subheading "Yolanda," the character from whose perspective the story is narrated. Yolanda's name will appear above the text on every odd-numbered page of that chapter. However, even the subheadings can, as seen at least in one instance, mislead the reader. The third chapter of the novel, titled "The Four Girls," with the subheading "Carla, Yolanda, Sandra, Sofía," is actually told from the mother's point of view, as she reflects on various comic, dramatic, tragic, and bittersweet moments in her daughters' lives. The reader, then, has to remain aware that in actuality the subheadings reveal whom the chapters are about, and they don't always coincide with the narrative point of view.

For nearly half the chapters, Alvarez opts for the third-person point of view, most of these in the third-person limited. Each of the four García sisters is the focal point at least once from the third-person limited viewpoint, with the exception of Yolanda, who receives the lion's share of the attention in the narrative. In this manner, Alvarez allows herself to explore the actions of each sister more fully, as well as the meaning and the consequences of these actions. An interesting use of the third-person perspective is found in the chapter titled "Daughter of Invention," with the subheading "Mami, Papi, Yoyo." The point of view will shift in this chapter between the mother's and Yolanda's. The interplay illustrates how, at the conclusion of the chapter, the mother will pass on the torch of creativity to her daughter, who is on her way to becoming a writer.

Seven of the novel's chapters are written from the first-person point of view. In the chapter titled "A Regular Revolution," with the subheading "Carla, Sandi, Yoyo, Fifi," Alvarez employs the seldom-used perspective of the first-person plural. It is an ingenious ploy that allows the four García sisters to view events from a unified front. In other words, they all think alike about the events narrated in this chapter. That is, until one of the sisters, Fifi, breaks away from the group when she is sent to live on the island in an effort to protect her from American vices. From this moment on, the "we" of the narrative becomes the sisters minus Fifi. As several months pass and the sisters are finally reunited on the island, the "we" of the narrative, the combined voice of the remaining three sisters, acts in opposition to Fifi and her total assimilation into the island's culture. This split in the first-person plural narrative voice highlights the wide gap in perspectives between the three sisters who remained in the United States, and the sister who has blended into the Latin-American culture. In the end, "A Regular Revolution" hinted at in the chapter's title, consists of the efforts of the three sisters to deprogram Fifi. They form a united "revolutionary" front that takes drastic steps to save the youngest sister from an unbalanced relationship that the collective voice ("we") deems as oppressive towards women. By means of the unorthodox use of the first-person plural, and the subsequent split in the collective voice, Alvarez writes about gender wars without overtly preaching a feminist message.

In a different vein, the chapter, "The Blood of the Conquistadores," with the subheading "Mami, Papi, The Four Girls," is an interesting study in the use of multiple points of view. This chapter is the only one divided into two parts. In Part I, the point of view shifts from Carlos, the father, to Yolanda; from Yolanda to the mother, Laura; from Laura to two minor characters—Doña Tatica and Victor; from them to Carla and Sandi; it then shifts again to Laura; from Laura to Pupo and Checo (members of the Dictator's secret police); from them to Sandi; and in closing it once again returns to Carlos. The shifting third-person omniscient point of view mirrors the rapidly changing circumstances in the lives of the García family. In an accelerated sequence of events, they are forced to flee their country in order to save Carlos's life. The changes in viewpoints reflect the increasingly chaotic lives of the characters, which change drastically and forever in merely a matter of hours. Part II of the chapter switches to the first-person. Fifi takes control of the narrative with a great degree of urgency. As the youngest of the García sisters, Fifi wants to share with the reader her only remaining memories of her birthplace: the day the family left the island forever. Alvarez gains the reader's full sympathy as she allows the character whose roots were severed most drastically to narrate the final events that take place in the Garcías' island household. Telling the story of the family's last moments in their former country constitutes Fifi's only chance to let her island self be heard. The narrative is then turned over to Chucha, a Haitian maid, who also tells her story in the first-person. A practitioner of the voodoo religion, she relates an eerie tale of a lifeless, tomb-like house. However, the spirits of the former owners still remain. The Garcías have left their island souls behind and are on their way to become citizens of a new— yet in Chucha's vision—emotionally dead country.

The three eldest sisters narrate the last four chapters of the novel using the first-person point of view. Each of them recollects an episode of their childhood on the island. In the final chapter, however, the point of view reveals an important key to the novel's entire narrative. Throughout the course of the work, Yolanda's viewpoint emerges as the most persistent. Yolanda is the only character who uses the first-person voice more than once. In fact, she uses the first-person viewpoint in five of the novel's fifteen chapters. The closing chapter reveals that it has, in fact, been Yolanda who has controlled the narrative all along. She has invented the viewpoints of all the other characters. She has put words into their mouths, which we later find causes much resentment and is a major feature in the first chapter of Alvarez's third novel, ¡Yo!. And so, the reader is left to wonder about the magic inherent in the Dominican-American's use of the point of view. It constitutes, indeed, a formidable narrative sleight of hand.

CHARACTER DEVELOPMENT

Traditionally, characterization, or the development of a character, is achieved by way of the traits with which an author endows each character and the manner in which the character puts these traits to work. In order to have a "well-rounded" character, the novelist must show all four sides of her or him. These sides are of a general nature, (gender, nationality, region of the world the character is from, social class, associates, etc.), a physical nature, a personal nature (traits that distinguish individuals from those like them; i.e., brave, selfish, sincere, etc.), and of an emotional nature (love, hate, patriotism, fear, etc.). The novelist must combine insight and richness in order to achieve good characterization.

The richness will come from making use of the character traits that form the identity of a protagonist. The insight comes from the novelist's knowledge of what her leading characters want from life.

In *How the García Girls Lost Their Accents*, each member of the García family, the novel's leading characters, has at least one chapter that helps define her or him. However, these characters are also defined by how other characters perceive them. The character development of the García sisters is panoramic. In other words, the reader sees them develop from childhood to adulthood. Or, in this particular case, in reverse chronological order, which can be disorienting.

Yolanda is the first central character the narrative introduces. She is also the novel's most fully developed character. Her identity, her concept of self, is fragmented, as evidenced by all of her names: Yolanda, Yo, Yoyo, and Joe. From the onset of the novel, Yolanda is out of place with the language and culture of her homeland. Her appearance and dress is different from her same-aged relatives. Yolanda is on the island in search of her place in the world as well as of her identity. She is uncertain as to where she belongs and where she will find happiness—whether in the United States or on the island. As she blows out the candles of her welcome-home cake, Yolanda begins to reflect back on the turbulent lives of the García sisters. It has been twenty-nine years since they left their birthplace for the United States. She fervently wishes to discover that the island is truly her home. Thus, the reader learns that displacement, the feeling of never knowing where one belongs, is central to Yolanda's character.

Yolanda considers herself a poet ("The Four Girls"). However, she is in the midst of experiencing writer's block as well as a deep sense of frustration over her career. Yolanda's desire to become a writer manifested itself at an early age ("Daughter of Invention"). In fact, it is her difficulty with her Americanization that leads to this ambition. Yolanda wants to make her mark in the world, and she chooses the written word, in a language other than her native one, to do so. In this instance she is selected, precisely because of her ability to express herself well, to give a speech honoring teachers. But at this point in her life, in elementary school, she is more preoccupied with her accent, about how it makes her different, than with the task of writing the speech. The accent, of course, is the running metaphor throughout the novel for being an outsider in the United States.

Alvarez provides the reader with an opportunity to learn more about Yolanda by contrasting her with her lover, John, who is one hundred percent American ("Joe"). She is impulsive, artistic, and emotional. He is rational, calculating, and distant. The scene that best provides us with a contrast takes place when Yolanda finds a list John has made of the pros and cons of remaining with Yolanda or returning to his wife. When Yolanda discovers, through a rhyme game in which he is unable to access her Spanish-language thoughts, that the cultural gap between her lover and her is too wide to bridge, she has a nervous breakdown and is interned in a psychiatric hospital. Fortunately, however, the reader also witnesses how she begins to heal from the ordeal.

Yolanda suffers from considerable guilt over some of the stories she told during her childhood ("The Blood of the Conquistadores"). She fears the repercussions her family may experience after she tells a general in Trujillo's army that her father owns a gun. The revelation that she informed the general of this sends the family into a panic and she feels responsible, in her young mind, for placing her father in danger. Because of this, she wishes for her own death. She learns the hard way, and at an early age, that the telling of stories can be a serious, even deadly, business. This crucial moment in Yolanda's development as a character will later be explored in greater depth and play a major role in Alvarez's third novel, ¡Yo!.

Yolanda, however, was destined, since childhood, to become a storyteller. Scheherazade's story inspires her ("The Human Body"). From reading *The Arabian Nights,* Yolanda learns that one can survive by telling stories. As she is trading corporeal secrets with her male cousin, the children are discovered while hiding in the garden shed, a spot forbidden to them. Yolanda quickly invents the story of one of Trujillo's soldiers passing through the yard and thus diverts the attention of the adults. At the conclusion of this episode, the anatomical man her cousin had received as a gift lays broken, and Yolanda is unable to piece it back together. Through this metaphor, then, the reader sees that Yolanda has lost her innocence. She has become a storyteller: a manipulator of facts, a teller of lies, and a creator of fiction. The incident constitutes an important rite of passage in her development as a character.

In the novel's last chapter, "The Drum," the reader travels back to the genesis of Yolanda's development as a character. Her removal of the kitten, her tossing it into the bushes, and the subsequent nightmares form the foundation of her existential displacement and of her need to purge her demons through storytelling. These memories, all of them collected in *How the García Girls Lost Their Accents,* haunt her and obligate her to become an artist in order to make sense of the tumultuous course of her life. As we can see, Yolanda's development makes it imperative for her to be the storyteller, the Scheherazade, of the García sisters.

In comparison to Yolanda, the other characters in the novel are much less developed, much less well-rounded. Of course, no other character compares to Yolanda in terms of his or her importance to the story. The remaining characters will be discussed by order of appearance. The narrative first introduces the youngest of the García sisters, Sofía, also known as Fifi, in the chapter titled "The Kiss." Sofía is portrayed as the most independent and rebellious of the sisters. We observe this in her troubled relationship with her father. She, unlike the other sisters, does not attempt to please him, but rather, she sets her own standards and expectations for living. At times these standards stand in defiance to his. The sensuous kiss that closes "The Kiss" shows Sofía at her most rebellious. It is a segment that shocks the reader. But what the kiss intends to demonstrate is that Sofía will go to any length to rebel against her father, even if it means humiliating him with an incestuous and arousing kiss that is performed in a very public setting: his birthday party.

Sofía, true to her namesake, Sophia, the Greek goddess of wisdom, is the wisest of the García sisters. Why? Because she is the only one who has learned to be truly happy with herself. She has the least amount of formal education, but she compensates for this by being the most contented of the family. She is happily married to a German chemist and they have given her father his only male descendant. This child has become Carlos's pride and joy. But Sofía wasn't always so level-headed. Opting to stay on the island as punishment for having claimed to be the owner of a plastic bag containing marijuana, she accepts a second exile because she wants to increase her bonds with her island heritage ("A Regular Revolution"). She does this, she says, because she is unhappy with her life in the United States. After a few months on the island, Sofía, overreacting to her sense of displacement, totally assimilates into the island culture. She is literally transformed into a young Latin American woman—emotionally and physically. She lets her macho boyfriend thoroughly dominate her. This infuriates her sisters, who plot to have their mother discover the physical intensity that characterizes the relationship between Sofía and the young man. In the end, Sofía is taken back to the United States. But her relationship with her sisters will never be the same. She will stand apart from the older ones and, as a result, she will not be the sweet, docile daughter and sister she once was. In essence, this episode marks the beginning of her rebelliousness—a rebelliousness that is later, as we have seen, directed toward her father.

Since Sofía is the youngest of the four sisters, and still a toddler when her family is forced to leave the island, she has precious few recollections of what her life was like there. In Part II of the chapter "The Blood of the Conquistadores," Sofía insists on taking over the narrative because, as she tells the reader, the day that the family left the island is the only memory she has of their lives there. Furthermore, most of these memories are really bits and pieces put together from what others have said about that day. Thus the reader observes that Sofía has the most tenuous ties to her heritage. She is, then, the sister who least suffers from cultural displacement. This makes her the most Americanized and, as a result, the one who reconciles most quickly with her American identity, with her life in the United States.

When the reader first learns about Sandra, better known as Sandi, she has been a patient in a psychiatric hospital following a nervous breakdown ("The Four Girls"). Like Cervantes's character, Don Quixote, whom she misquotes, Sandi has suffered a mental collapse from reading excessively while attending graduate school. Her mother also comments that in addition to this, Sandi's choice of men may have something to do with her condition. As a result of her breakdown, Sandi has lost touch with her humanity, firmly believing that she is turning into a monkey. Later in the same chapter, Sandi is home, out of the clinic, but on antidepressants. Based on the way in which she reacts to her sisters' comments, the reader concludes that Sandi, as an adult, is hypersensitive, hard on herself, and does not take criticism well.

Sandi suffers from an inferiority crisis stemming, in large part, from her being the second of four sisters who are close in age ("Floor Show"). There is nothing remarkable about "the second daughter of a second daughter" ("Still Lives" 241). The family does, though, discover that Sandi has a talent for painting. In order to properly develop her talent, the Garcías hope to place Sandi under the tutelage of a German artist, Doña Charito, who married a talented painter, a native of the island who mysteriously disappeared years before. The García clan, though, insists that all of the sisters and their cousins also attend the painting lessons. This reinforces Sandi's notion that there is nothing exceptional about her. During the very first lesson, Sandi soon grows impatient with the basics of using a brush and she expresses her artistic soul by painting a cat without the teacher's consent. This causes the teacher to remove Sandi from class. Sandi shows an inclination for blackmail when she looks around the house hoping to find a secret that she can use against Doña Charito. Indeed, she discovers that Doña Charito's husband, a gifted but insane artist, is kept in chains in a studio. However, Sandi pays a hefty price for her discovery. She falls from where she is perched observing him and breaks her arm. Her recovery takes one year because the bone doesn't heal properly, has to be broken again, reset, and recast. This childhood trauma turns Sandi, as the narrative states, into the inward-looking, sullen, whiny person she is in adulthood.

Moving on to the last of the sisters, Carla, the eldest, is the least defined and the least developed character. Primarily she is judgmental of others. Carla and her husband, both psychologists, come across as obnoxious during the dinner-table scene in their whispered remarks to each other regarding the personalities of the other sisters ("The Four Girls"). The anecdote the mother tells about Carla and the red sneakers also reveals her stubbornness, which follows her into adulthood. Carla is portrayed as probing and analytical as well. She is constantly attempting to look into the human mind, into the inner beings and motivations of others. Her profession, of course, requires her to do so in order to help her patients. Nevertheless, with her sisters she is not helpful, but rather, merely critical.

As the oldest of the sisters, however, Carla is the one who experiences the most significant trauma because of the family's exile. From the onset, she suffers more severely from cultural displacement than her siblings. Carla wishes that she could return home. She feels that she has lost everything in her move to the United States. One manner in which her displacement is exhibited is in her strong fear that she will never master English. She feels inadequate and her immigrant father further embarrasses her, particularly with his accent. In the school she attends, a different one than her sisters, Carla is the object of racist and sexist remarks ("Trespass"). She is the victim of physical violence, as well. To make matters worse, once, on her walk home, an adult male exposes himself. Later, when the police question Carla, her insecurities are aggravated. These incidents exacerbate her cultural displacement, affecting her self-concept. However, they also lead Carla to become a psychologist in order to understand human behavior, her own included. Still, as stated earlier, as a character Carla remains the least developed of the sisters.

On the other hand, the mother, Laura, or Mami, is, after Yolanda, the novel's most developed character. She is the family storyteller, and it becomes obvious that Yolanda inherited this gift from her. In the dinner scene, everyone at the table is fully engaged as Laura tells the anecdote of Carla's red sneakers ("The Four Girls"). In the course of the novel, we learn that the mother is a wonderfully humorous, albeit unintentional, transformer of proverbs and expressions. But she is far from being a relaxed character. Due to her island upbringing, Laura is considerably more conservative than her "Americanized" daughters. When telling the story of how Sofía and her husband came together, she changes the details to fit her moral standards, which condemn premarital sex. In spite of this, as the family listens attentively while Mami tells their stories, the reader observes how she is the glue that holds them together.

In spite of her conservatism, the mother's emerging feminism is evident. Laura has been gaining greater independence via her enrollment in college courses ("A Regular Revolution"). Later, when she learns that at least one of her daughters had been experimenting with marijuana, she decides to handle the disciplining on her own, without consulting her husband. But Laura has always been her own person. In fact, for a time she excessively concentrates on her personal projects ("Daughter of Invention"). The sisters resent their mother who, in pursuit of her inventions, has neglected to help them adjust to their new country. The mother's self-absorption stems from her need to prove herself in the United States. Back on the island, her surname was all she needed to establish her worth, but in the United States she has become obsessed about proving her intelligence, her ability, and her desire to succeed. Her character development, then, revolves around the pain of her cultural displacement and how, in spite of this, she tries to be the best mother and wife possible.

Carlos, the father, stands alone as the family patriarch and as the only central character that is male. As a Latin American, he subscribes to the supremacy of men within the family. Nevertheless, the women in his household overwhelm him. He masks his profound disappointment at never having a son with the recurring remark: "Good bulls sire cows." As a male, he marks his territory. The daughters visit for his birthday but are told to leave their husbands and boyfriends at home ("The Kiss"). He feels so alone as the only man in the family that, although estranged from Sofía, he is proud of her because she gave him a grandson, his first male descendant.

Shortly after the Garcías arrive in the U.S., Carlos is portrayed as a shell-shocked refugee ("Floor Show"). He exhibits concern not only for the tense political situation back home, but also for the considerable personal debt he has incurred with Dr. Fanning, the physician who sponsored the family's move to the United States. While out to dinner with the Fannings, Carlos feels his sense of honor compromised because his sponsor is paying for everyone. His pride has also been affected because it was Dr. Fanning who secured him a job as a hotel physician. Furthermore, Sandi notices how her father, normally a confident individual, is extremely insecure around "independent" American women, notably so in the case of Mrs. Fanning. Earlier in the chapter, as the family hails the cab that will take them from their apartment to the restaurant, Alvarez superimposes the difficulty that Carlos has communicating in English with the driver upon the prestigious social standing he used to enjoy on the island. It offers us a stark contrast in which we see how far the father's fortunes have fallen with his immigration, and of how much he will have to struggle to find his place in his adoptive homeland.

The chapter "The Blood of the Conquistadores" takes the reader straight into the heart of Carlos's plight. Security forces discover the plot that he has become involved in to overthrow the island's dictator. Carlos has become, then, metaphorically, a marked man. If he remains on the island he is certain to be imprisoned, tortured, and, perhaps, executed. This incident greatly influences the early years of his life in the United States. It is not until much later, with his daughters grown and he a grandfather, that Carlos at last rids himself of the fear of living in a police state at the mercy of a dictator. Ultimately, his family gives him the strength to adjust to a new language, a new culture, and a new country.

As we have seen, the structure of *How the García Girls Lost Their Accents* obliges the reader to pay close attention to the development of the characters. Like pieces of a puzzle, we have to find the images and recollections of our reading that fit into the proper place to help define a character. Although some of the characters remain underdeveloped—most notably in the case of Carla—we come to understand the painful effects of cultural displacement, of having to leave home, family, language, and customs behind in order to carve out a new, and at times difficult, existence. Through it all, however, in spite of the hardships, Alvarez's characters retain a certainty that their destiny, their final selves, even at the novel's end, remain in a state of development, of actualization. Even in the first chapter—which, again, chronologically is the last—the reader encounters the central character, Yolanda, asking herself the questions that have haunted her and her sisters ever since childhood: Who am I, and where do I belong?

LITERARY DEVICE: THE INTERPLAY OF LANGUAGES

Beginning with the novel's title, *How the García Girls Lost Their Accents*, the reader expects a cross-cultural story that also promises to be humorous. We can also assume, again based on the title, that the plot deals

with the acculturation of "the García Girls." In reading the novel, the
reader will be gratified with how Alvarez meets these expectations.
However, we cannot, by any means, say that everything in the novel is
humorous. In fact, Alvarez is very adept at using humor to probe into
serious, sometimes troublesome human issues. So, in spite of the novel's
title, the text will provoke the reader into thinking about many problems
that are not just related to the Garcías and their culture, but that also are
universal in nature. Nevertheless, losing one's accent is, indeed, a metaphor for the acculturation process—something that intimately affects the
novel's main characters. The family's difficulties with their new language
accentuate their pain in becoming "Americans." In fact, many of the
chapters deal with the sisters' experiences with linguistic and cultural
displacement.

For the most part, it is through Yolanda that the reader experiences
the joys and the disappointments involved in becoming American, an
experience that is inextricably linked to learning the English language.
Yolanda gleefully states that English during her freshman year in college
had become like a "party favor"—she discovers the meaning of an unknown word by "cracking" a dictionary (87). Although this statement
leads the reader to expect that from this point forward all of Yolanda's
experiences in her new language are pleasant, it is quite the contrary.
Much to her frustration, Yolanda still sees herself as a foreigner. For
instance, in conversing quietly with others, she considers her tendency
to whisper in complete sentences a habit that betrays her foreignness
(90). Also, when she writes a sonnet with Rudy, the words, phrases, and
images he inserts into the poem are full of double meanings. He has to
explain them to her because she is unable to grasp the alternate meanings
since she grew up in another culture, another language. Furthermore,
the manner in which her classmates laugh upon reading the verses accentuates her sense of alienation. These experiences solidify her feelings
of being an outsider, thus reinforcing her feelings of inadequacy.

Carla, the eldest of the García sisters, is also subjected to the same
feelings early in her life in the United States. For instance, Carla ponders
on the double significance of "trespass." Both meanings bewilder her.
On the one hand, in the context of the novel, it means to invade another's
property. Carla, however, based on having learned "The Lord's Prayer"
in her new language, interprets it as to commit an offense or to sin. In
her confusion she becomes certain that she will never master English.
Later, the narrative reflects on Carla's frustration with both the language
and the culture of her new country. She feels utterly alone, certain that

she will always be an outsider, that the United States will never be her home. At this point in the narrative, when Carla is feeling most vulnerable and alone, Alvarez introduces the exposure incident to reinforce the hostility that at times underlies the Americanization process. It is a testimony to Carla's strength of character and to her intelligence that she goes on not only to master the language, but also to earn a doctorate in psychology.

The Garcías are lost between languages and cultures—Spanish and English, American and Latin American. The title of the novel's first chapter, "Antojos," indicates that the experience that awaits the reader will, at times, be bilingual and bicultural. Indeed, the novel does speak of the joys and, yes, the pains of not belonging entirely in one world or the other. The sisters, to varying degress, all suffer from cultural displacement, and the bulk of their displacement revolves around the issue of language. The sisters grow up speaking Spanish. Then, because of circumstances beyond their control, they are obliged to learn English—an experience that causes them considerable trauma. In "Antojos," we encounter Yolanda as a thirty-nine year old who now laments her loss of Spanish. She feels awkward speaking the language of her childhood. She has mastered English, but at the cost of losing her once native ability in her mother tongue. Alvarez ably mines this feature of the immigrant experience: the duality, linguistic and cultural, of living on the hyphen, of being a Dominican-American, and by extension a Hispanic-American. While on the island, Yolanda recalls a conversation with a Spanish-speaking poet. Their exchange makes her doubt if Spanish is still her native language. To her amazement, and regret, Yolanda realizes that she has never had a love affair involving the Spanish language and, furthermore, she doubts that if she did her thoughts would be in that language (13).

Later in the same chapter, when Yolanda's vehicle gets a flat tire while far from the main road, she reverts to English after two *campesinos*, or farm laborers, approach her offering their help. In fear, Spanish fails her. English, then, comes to represent safety, her way out of the predicament. She has become, for all intents and purposes, an American—much to her sorrow as she continues searching for her place in the world. She feels that she has moved too far from her roots, that she has strayed from her heritage.

Language, or in the case of the García sisters, the gap that exists between Spanish and English, also affects their relationships with men. This is in evidence in the doomed relationship between Yolanda and her lover, John ("Joe"). In large part, her relationship with John is destined to fail because of their linguistic differences. As Yolanda plays the rhyme game with John, he cannot match her poetic sensibilities, not in English and much less in Spanish. The reader observes how the distance between them grows when he is unable to traverse across the gap separating English from Spanish. As Yolanda becomes frustrated with his inability to rhyme "Yo," she reaches into her mother tongue to find the world *cielo*, in English, "sky." John's monolinguism convinces Yolanda that he will never be able to fully penetrate her world. Language is the gap their relationship cannot bridge. In fact, her sense of self is so wrapped up in language that she deeply resents having acquired several of John's speech traits (73). The rupture in their relationship takes place when Yolanda blames John for provoking her to use the word "fuck," her least favorite word in the English language (76–77). Shortly after Yolanda's final argument with John, she begins to babble. Everything she says is nonsensical. Because of this her family interns her in a psychiatric institution for treatment. She later tells her parents that her relationship with John has ended because they were no longer speaking the same language. In her breakdown, Yolanda, the poet, has damaged her own vital relationship to language. Words as essential to her craft as "love" and "alive" now inflict great pain (82). The chapter does, however, conclude on a positive note when she begins to rediscover her love of language.

The most notable aspect regarding Alvarez's employment of the interplay of languages as a literary device, however, is her use of the gap between Spanish and English for humorous effect. This is mainly achieved through the mother's use, or more accurately, misuse, of proverbs and English-language sayings. This feature of *How the García Girls Lost Their Accents* is bound to delight virtually every reader. Proverbs are for the most part learned during adolescence, and since Laura lived this part of her life in the Spanish-speaking world, her adult mind is not quite able to grasp the significance of the subtle yet hilarious variations she performs on these English-language expressions. Sometimes she combines two different sayings that to her "foreign" ear sound perfectly fine, but do not quite reflect their proper usage. For instance, while describing a crowded bus, Laura states: "It was more sardines in a can than you could shake a stick at" (49). She also slightly transforms other expressions such as when she refers to Sandi's Nordic looks as "peaches and ice cream skin" (52). The chapter "Daughter of Invention" has the greatest inventory of the mother's mixed metaphors, which indeed provide the novel with its most humorous moments.

How the García Girls Lost Their Accents also contains a significant amount of toying with proverbs in translation—from Spanish to English. The inclusion of these proverbs represents Alvarez's nod to her bilingual readers, who constitute a large portion of her audience. Spanish expressions such as *No hay moros en la costa* (86), *Con paciencia y calma, hasta un burro sube la palma* (138), *Mi casa es su casa* (203), and *En boca cerrada no entran moscas* (209) appear to the delight of those who fully understand the Hispanic language and culture. Yet another humorous play between languages takes place when the girls entertain themselves with the names of relatives by translating them (111). Thus we see how the Dominican-American author ably mines the gap between languages for dramatic, as well as humorous, effect.

THEMATIC ISSUES

In *How the García Girls Lost Their Accents*, the Dominican-American writer explores a wide range of themes central to the immigration experience. The García family, as is the case with all immigrants, encounters a reality vastly different than their own. The differences, linguistic and cultural, oblige them to devise strategies with which to cope with situations that are both new and bewildering. More importantly, however, it obliges the Garcías, individually, to confront their sense of self, to question who they have been their entire lives, and to consider carefully who they are to become.

Ranking high on the list of themes Alvarez explores is that of Americanization. The novel can, to a great extent, be considered a treatise on this subject. After all, it is the difficulty Yolanda experiences with her Americanization that has turned her into a writer. The pain of being different, of being an outsider, compels her to document her existence in order to give it legitimacy. As mentioned often in the section on character development, all of the novel's personages at one point or another deal with the hardships involved in becoming an American. The frequently repeated phrases of "straightening out" or "losing their accents," support this theme. The father, often when his daughters anger him, will bring up how much he had paid for their education so that they can speak without an accent, so that they can fit into American society. He believes that his daughters should exhibit greater gratitude for his sacrifice, as he provided them with the appropriate schooling to assimilate quickly into their adoptive homeland. On the other hand, the sisters are

often embarrassed by their father's accent. One needs only to listen to
him speak in order to know that he is not, in origin, an American. His
accent betrays him, and this stifles his daughters' desire as adolescents
to blend in seamlessly into their new country.

A theme apart from Americanization, but closely related to it, is the
theme of cultural displacement—in other words, how a person feels
awkward in an alien setting. The chapter "The Rudy Elmenhurst Story"
provides the reader with a remarkably clear illustration of Yolanda
García's cultural displacement. Yolanda curses her immigrant roots
when the class erupts into laughter after reading the sonnet she co-
authored with Rudy. Because of her inability to grasp the double-
meaning behind several of the verses, she feels left out of the joke, very
much an outsider. When both her family and Rudy's arrive for parents'
weekend, the reader observes how cultural differences can manifest
themselves visually. Her parents' dress is exaggeratedly conservative, a
reflection of what is worn on these occasions in the old country. On the
other hand, the attire of Rudy's parents is casual and decidedly youthful.
The cultural differences are accentuated further when, after Rudy's parents learn that he is dating "a Spanish girl," they enthusiastically suggest
that he should take advantage of this opportunity to learn about people
of other cultures. To this, Yolanda quips: "It bothered me that they
should treat me like a geography lesson for their son" (98). Understand-
ably, after the breakup of her relationship with Rudy, Yolanda laments
that she will never find someone who will understand or appreciate her
biculturalism.

The move to the United States deeply affects the entire family. Their
struggle to become Americanized often frustrates them. The chapter "A
Regular Revolution" begins with the sisters' dismay after learning of
their father's decision to reside permanently in the United States. The
García sisters argue that they feel that they have not gotten the best that
their new country has to offer, and they have little hope that they will
ever do so. Their difficulty in adjusting to their surroundings is evident,
this in spite of already having resided in the United States for several
years. When Sofía decides to remain on the island as punishment, her
stated reason is that life in the United States isn't making her happy.
Later, when the other sisters learn of Sofía's total re-assimilation into the
island culture, including a visual transformation that has her looking like
an S.A.P., a "Spanish-American Princess," Carla, then a budding psychologist, comments that Sofía's "repatriation" is "a borderline schizoid
response to traumatic cultural displacement" (117–118). Thus, the sense

of not belonging in the United States can cause enough trauma for a character to completely transform herself.

The novel's briefest chapter, "Snow," superimposes Yolanda's new country, her new language, and her fear of the unknown onto the Cuban Missile Crisis of 1962. In the end, because Yolanda had never seen snow before, she confuses all the new sensory and cultural input to declare the first snowflakes of the year to be the beginning of a much anticipated nuclear attack. Her statement strikes panic among her American classmates. Her declaration, though, is not made out of malice, but, rather, it constitutes a manifestation of her cultural displacement formulated in a context entirely unfamiliar to her. Thus, in this chapter, Yolanda's Americanization is seen as something fearful yet, at the same time, wondrous. Eventually the members of the García family adjust to their new homeland to the best of their capabilities. But some characters, like Yolanda, will never fully acquire a sense of place, a sense of belonging to either culture.

The essence of the generational conflicts in the García family is defined in the chapter "Daughter of Invention." Here, the narrative states that the problem between the sisters and their parents resides in the fact that the younger generation wanted to become American and the elders would have none of it. Clashes between generations are a universal theme. However, among immigrants, the differences in cultural perceptions can become magnified, and at times heated, as they adapt to the different values and standards of conduct of their new homelands.

A delicate subject that Alvarez broaches in *How the García Girls Lost Their Accents* is racism. Racism is the notion that one's race, one's ethnicity, is superior to another. It can be expressed overtly and, as in most instances, subtly. Surprisingly, the first appearance of racism does not have any of the Garcías as victims but, rather, the attitude rears its head within the family. People of white European ancestry have enjoyed a privileged position in Latin American society. Historically, and still today, descendants of white Europeans have benefited socially, economically, and politically because of their racial ancestry. This advantage works to the detriment of other populations, such as the indigenous, the black, and the mestizo (which comprises the majority in Latin America, being of mixed race: indigenous and European). In the García family, it is first Carlos who cannot suppress his preference for his grandson, a preference based in large part on the child's blond hair and blue eyes. Carlos states that his grandson's birth has brought "good blood" into the family lineage (26–27). By "good blood," the father refers to the in-

fant's racial features—in other words, to the European features he has
inherited from Otto. Carlos considers Otto's Germanic origins an improvement in the family's gene pool. In placing a higher value on the
infant's light complexion, the father denigrates the family's mestizo heritage. Laura, the mother, also strongly favors her European heritage. She
is proud of her Swedish ancestry; a preference based solely on race. Race,
then, constitutes a social commodity. The fairer the skin of the family,
the higher they rank in society.

Ironically, the incidents detailing the Garcías' racial preferences take
place many years after they emigrated from the island. The parents seem
to have forgotten the racial prejudice they and their daughters experienced shortly after their arrival to the United States. It is through the
Garcías as recent immigrants that Alvarez more closely explores the issue
of racism. At times, because of the family's Latin American heritage, the
sisters are thought of in stereotypical terms. Rudy expresses that he pursued Yolanda because he thought that she would turn out to be a "hot-
blooded Spanish woman" (99). In other words, he pursued her believing
that Latinas are passionate and uninhibited in bed. But the Garcías are
also subjected to more virulent manifestations of racism. In the chapter
"Trespass," the boys on the playground torment Carla with the epithet
of "spic," and they also make fun of her accent, which, as we have seen,
is her worst fear as an immigrant (153). In the chapter "Floor Show,"
racism is presented at its starkest. It is embodied in the character of the
old woman who lives directly below the family in their first apartment
building in the United States. The elderly woman is offended by the
smell of the Garcías's food, by their voices, and in particular because
they do not speak English. Her hostility toward the Garcías moves her
to shout "Spics! Go back to where you came from!" (171). The building's
superintendent is a sympathetic Puerto Rican. However, he can only
advise the family to resign themselves to the abuse. He sadly informs
the Garcías that they will soon get used to it because that is the way
things are in their new country. This is, by far, the most explicit instance
of racism found in *How the García Girls Lost Their Accents*. On a positive
note, however, in the same chapter, Sandi, through her experience with
the meals and the performers in the Spanish restaurant, learns to feel
pride in her Hispanic heritage. She observes that Hispanic culture is
appreciated and valued by many people in the United States.

Racism, however, is not exclusive to the United States. It also surfaces
during their lives on the island. In "The Blood of the Conquistadors,"
among Fifi's few recollections is the contempt and fear that Chucha, the

Haitian maid, provokes among the other maids because of her blackness. Alvarez contrasts Chucha with another maid named Nivea (a Spanish synonym for "white"). Nivea, a woman with a far lighter complexion than Chucha, looks down upon the darkest of the family's maids—first because of Chucha's pigmentation and second because Chucha is Haitian rather than Dominican. However, Nivea also fears Chucha because she is a practitioner of voodoo—a religion closely associated with Afro-Caribbean culture. Racism in *How the García Girls Lost Their Accents* transcends borders and cultures. It is, unfortunately, a universal theme. It not only manifests itself in the lives of the García family in the United States, but also in the world they left behind.

Very much related to racism, Latin America suffers from profound and conflictive class differences. It constitutes a problem as endemic and pernicious as racism. The ruling classes in Latin America have, historically and at present, imposed their will upon the poor. In "Antojos," beginning in the third paragraph, the reader encounters the stark contrast that exists between the ruling class and the poor. In this case it is exemplified by the presence of the children's nursemaids "who sit on stools at the far end of the patio, a phalanx of starched white uniforms" (3). Yolanda's relatives are wealthy enough to afford a nursemaid for each of their children. These women are relegated to the margins, literally and metaphorically. The starched white uniforms rob them of their individuality, and they are subjected to the whims of several generations of wealthy people. Later in the narrative, one of the maids from the kitchen staff, as indicated by her black uniform, docilely looks downward at her clasped hands in a *"gesture of pleading"* (italics Alvarez's) as one of the aunts scolds her (4).

In a separate incident, another of the aunts, Tía Flor, complains about the hired help and about how their quality worsens every day. In a classic example of the magnitude of the problem of class differences, she complains specifically about the chauffeur who allowed her car to run out of gas in "the middle of a university barrio" (5). There is no scenario that could strike greater fear in the heart of the ruling elite than to be trapped helplessly in a university neighborhood. College campuses around Latin America, in particular the poorer, public institutions of higher education, are hotbeds of revolution. This is where many young people first become engaged in bitter and often violent class struggles. Thus, Tía Flor found herself, thanks to her chauffeur's neglect, stranded in the heart of enemy territory.

Later, a maid is metaphorically stripped of her humanity. The reader observes this when Altagracia, who has been in the family's service a long time, is called upon to serve as a human dictionary—in particular a dictionary that specializes in the lexicon of the rural poor. This takes place when an aunt sends for Altagracia so that she can illustrate for Yolanda what the word *antojo* signifies among uneducated country people. When asked to explain the meaning of the word, the maid replies: "U'te que sabe" ("You're the one to know"). Her reply indicates how the poor submit in everything, including language, to the authority of the rich.

Although Yolanda, in her egalitarian, American mind, tries to rise above the prejudices underlying class differences, there is nothing she can do to change how Latin American society has evolved over centuries. She discovers this after she is on her own, driving a car borrowed from her family. When Yolanda stops at a *cantina* looking for guavas, the owner, a woman, apologizes to her because the grandson hides from the Americanized islander. But it is not Yolanda's American qualities that brings about the boy's timidity; it is, as the woman states, that he is not used to "being among people"—meaning people of wealth, the rich (15). When Yolanda's car gets a flat tire while she is alone, off the main road and far from help, she panics at the sight of two *campesinos*. Not only is her fear gender-based, but it is also based on the prejudices she hasn't been able to elude regarding class differences. She fears that the two men will harm her. But she wouldn't have feared them had they looked and acted as if they belonged to the upper class. Yolanda's strategy to protect herself is to speak only in English, hoping her American identity will save her from the two *campesinos*. However, as an added measure she mentions the last name of some relatives who live nearby, knowing that the name will automatically cast apprehension in the hearts of the men who know that if they harm a wealthy woman there will be serious consequences. Thus the reader discovers that Yolanda is also subject to prejudices based on class differences. The chapter's ending, with the image of the Palmolive soap billboard hovering above the impoverished *cantina* where Yolanda has stopped looking for guavas, serves as a final reminder of the racial and class differences found on the island. Simply put, there are those who can afford Palmolive soap and thus have a smiling, carefree life—as illustrated by the pose of the woman on the billboard—and then there's the majority of the islanders who live far below that lifestyle.

The second chapter that explores the theme of class differences is "An American Surprise." Although narrated from Carla's point of view, the story constitutes a case study on class differences centered around Gladys, the youngest of the maids. Gladys is a colorful, carefree character who dreams of living in New York City. Among her list of favorite saints is the powerful American saint—ironically, the Statue of Liberty—who will help her achieve her dreams. When Carlos, the father, returns from a trip to the United States, he brings each daughter a gift: toy banks that perform tricks while putting the coins away. These banks seem magical to Gladys. The maid is an integral part of the scene where the father demonstrates how the banks operate. In Gladys's innocent eyes, the banks are a miracle. It is Carlos, the father, who expresses the ruling class condescending attitude toward Gladys, and by extension toward all other maids, when he states in the collective third-person plural: "They're like children . . ." (266). He scoffs at her innocence, and obviously considers others of the working class to be equally simple-minded. Gladys, enamored with Carla's bank, offers to buy it. Carla, already bored with the gift, gives the bank to Gladys on the condition that she not tell anyone. When the parents notice that the bank is missing, they immediately suspect the maids of being thieves. After searching their quarters, they discover the bank in Gladys' possession. Gladys, bound by her word, does not tell them that it was a gift from Carla. And Carla, too young and fearful to tell the truth, does not clarify in time what actually took place. In a demonstration of the power that one social class exerts over another, Gladys is fired. The ruling class has protected its hegemony, or dominance, over the poor.

The last theme Alvarez tackles is that of Latin American politics, particularly the politics of the Dominican Republic during and after the dictatorship of Rafael Trujillo. Trujillo represents the second longest one-man rule in Latin America's turbulent history. He governed the country despotically from 1930 until his assassination in 1961. The Dominican dictator plays a vital role in Alvarez's second novel, *In the Time of the Butterflies*. In *How the García Girls Lost Their Accent*, however, politics is not a prominent theme. It is, though, featured in the novel's first chapter, "Antojos." In addition to presenting the university barrio, or neighborhood, as a dangerous, highly politicized zone, Alvarez also brings into the reader's mind Latin America's guerilla wars. She accomplishes this by the mere mention of the danger armed revolutionaries pose if one visits the island's mountainous region (10). Also, in terms of political themes, the reader needs to keep in mind the powerful metaphor of the Palmolive billboard, which represents the marriage between the island's ruling class and American enterprise.

With regard to Rafael Trujillo, throughout the novel one finds several references to Carlos's involvement in the plot to overthrow the dictator, and of how this led to his and his family's exile. The fear of the the the government's harsh reckoning with dissenters haunts the father for several years after his move to the United States. Already safe in the United States, he panics when his wife awakens him in the middle of the night. Startled, he believes that he is back on the island and the secret police have come for him ("Daughter of Invention" 139). Later, Yolanda reads a draft of the speech she wrote for the convocation honoring teachers. She reads the speech aloud while standing in front of the television as it broadcasts news of the war in Southeast Asia. The narrative reminds the reader, however, that just a few weeks before the news on television had been dominated by the 1965 Marine invasion of their homeland, the Dominican Republic. Superimposed on this, Yolanda's speech metaphorically calls for the student to destroy the teacher—inspired by a Walt Whitman poem and signifying that a student must improve upon what he or she learns from the teacher while at the same time retaining his or her individuality. The father interprets the metaphor to kill the teacher in an almost literal fashion. The consequences of speaking out against authority, a danger that he was fearful of on the island, leads him to destroy the lone copy of Yolanda's speech. In anger, she refers to him as *Chapita*, which was the dictator's hated nickname. In Yolanda's anger, the father and his nemesis are superimposed, becoming one and the same. It is a jolt for the father to be compared to the man who squelched his own freedom of speech. In regret, the father buys Yolanda an electric typewriter, a highly liberating gesture, which he gives to her as a gift. Thus the reader observes how the politics of the island reach far into their lives in the United States. The turbulence and instability of their homeland still haunt the Garcías.

The chapter "The Blood of the Conquistadores" is where the reader experiences the island's politics at their most fearful and dangerous. The chapter begins with political intrigue as the father hides from the members of Trujillo's secret police. As the police interrogate the mother, the narrative fills us in on certain facts about Dominican politics. For instance, we learn how Trujillo has food tasters, how other members of the García family fear imprisonment, and how one cousin went so far as to commit suicide in jail rather than betray his fellow dissenters while under torture. It is a harsh reality that sadly was true throughout this time in the island's history. The character of Victor—a CIA agent and American embassy attaché—embodies the most intriguing political feature of this chapter. He is the mastermind behind a failed plot to overthrow Trujillo. Although considered the family savior, Victor embodies U.S. foreign policy and practices at its most unsavory. When the call for help reaches him, Victor is in a bordello, having sex with an adolescent prostitute. He comes across as a cold, calculating, heartless man. His only goal is to expedite U.S. foreign policy, and he could care less about the people affected. He helps the Garcías out of a sense of duty, but there is no compassion behind his actions. In essence, Victor represents U.S. hegemony, or dominance, in Latin America.

A FEMINIST READING OF *HOW THE GARCÍA GIRLS LOST THEIR ACCENTS*

One of the trademarks of feminist criticism is its diversity. However, it can be said that all feminist criticism shares a common purpose: to expose the mechanisms upon which patriarchal society rests and continues to sustain itself. The ultimate aim of feminist inquiry is to transform social relations. Therefore the objective of feminist criticism is fundamentally a "political" one. Feminists advocate the transformation of society because of their belief that it operates to the advantage of men and serves their interests above all others. Ingrained in this belief as well is the notion that patriarchal society oppresses women.

Feminism, though, lacks a single, comprehensive definition. Therefore, feminist literary criticism also lacks a single distinctive methodology. At best, we can speak of feminisms. Each of these feminisms is engaged in the transformational critical practice described above. These feminisms operate across many disciplines—and they are often interdisciplinary in approach. Thus, feminist literary critics tend to borrow the methodological and conceptual tools of other fields that meet the needs of their work. Because of this methodological freedom, because the viewpoints of feminists are not grounded in a single, integrated theory, they have been able to explore a wide range of issues. As mentioned at the beginning of this section, diversity is the trademark of feminist studies.

In literature, feminist criticism simply asks the reader to remain mindful that the portrayals of women are often stereotypical and fail to reflect their reality. Latina feminists, following the example of black feminists, have helped overhaul the feminist agenda to include a more complex version of power relations—both within and outside the Latino culture. What readers need to ask themselves in a feminist reading are questions regarding the placement of women in a story; the image conveyed; the role that gender, race, and social class plays; the portrayal of the relationships between men and women; and the relationships between women.

First of all, a feminist critique would note that the novel's author is, obviously, a woman. An important feature for many feminist critics is to draw attention to women writers who create in the historically male-dominated world of literature. Second, it should be noted that Alvarez populates the novel primarily with women who, as the title indicates, undergo the process of acculturation into American society. Furthermore, the inclusion of the noun "girls" (as opposed to women) in the title can conceivably trigger debate among feminist critics that the characters have been rendered somewhat incomplete, not yet fully formed as people, as women. The fact is that the García sisters do, throughout the course of the narrative, struggle against sexism. Much of their struggle takes place in the male-dominated, patriarchal Latin American culture. But the reader must also keep in mind that the García sisters also struggle against racism and xenophobia—fear of foreigners—since they are never fully accepted in American society because of their minority/immigrant status.

When discussing Latin American and United States Latino culture, scholars often refer to the concept of machismo. Machismo is also an important focal point of feminist inquiry across a wide range of disciplines. Although the term originated in the study of Latin American society, it is not exclusive to this culture, as the concept has now extended into studies focusing on male power structures as well as on relationships that exert an inordinate amount of control over women's behavior. In essence, when referring to the concept of machismo, which has *macho*, Spanish for "male gender," as its root, it connotes strength, bravery, power, and importance. These qualities are viewed as those the ideal man possesses within a patriarchal society. Thus, in such a society, machismo becomes institutionalized. Women and female qualities are relegated to secondary status, deemed more suitable for childrearing and maintenance of the home. The man has the power and the authority to make decisions for the women under his protectorate. Men also attempt to control women's behavior. In a society characterized by machismo, women's voices have been silenced, their stories receive little or no attention. That is why the success of Julia Alvarez's writings, and those of other U.S. Latinas, have such great significance and resonate so strongly—they speak for an entire population that historically has been without voice. Herein lays the genuine triumph of the García sisters: their stories are heard. This constitutes a victory for Latinas, and by extension, for all women.

In the patriarchal society to which the sisters belong they have to struggle constantly against the dominance men have over women. In the chapter "A Regular Revolution," we find ourselves in the midst of a gender war. In fact, the "Revolution" to which the title refers is against Latin American patriarchal society. Fifi's boyfriend and cousin, Manuel, is the embodiment of machismo. The narrative describes him as a "tyrant." He does not allow Fifi to wear pants in public, talk to other men, nor to leave the house without his permission (120). He even attempts to discourage her from reading because women are not supposed to develop an intellect—their destinies are to become wives and mothers. Oddly enough, Fifi, who has become acculturated to the island's way of life, accepts Manuel's dominance with little or no resistance. Manuel's machismo and Fifi's acquiescence is what the other sisters plot their revolt against. Their desire is to free Fifi from subscribing to the codes of women's behavior as prescribed by Latin American culture. The problem is that Fifi and the women around her believe in the prevailing order. Thus, they comply with their mates' demands, however unreasonable and outmoded they may seem to the contemporary mind.

Carlos, the father, also subscribes to machismo. It is ingrained in him. He has grown up in the Latin American culture. Therefore, he views male dominance and control over the women in his care as the natural order of things. He considers himself the family patriarch, its undisputed master. As head of the family, it is Carlos, without consulting another family member, who makes the decision that the Garcías will remain in the United States permanently. Although this decision deeply affects the entire family, he alone has the right to make it. The women in his family are under his protectorate. His control over his daughters' lives is further evidenced in the chapter "The Kiss." In this chapter he demands that his daughters maintain the tradition of returning to their parental home to celebrate his birthday. However, he also insists that they come alone, without their husbands or mates. He wants to be the sole male, in essence marking his territory. He refers to the collective that his daughters constitute as his "harem;" an indication, albeit affectionate, that he considers them his property. His pride as a man, however, is affected by his failure to father a son, to produce a male heir. "Good bulls sire cows," he often says. However, the reader can grasp the hollowness behind the supposedly humorous statement. He receives some consolation in the male descendant that Fifi gives him. In this fashion, his patrimony is somewhat assured—although the surname, "García," is destined to end with his daughters' generation.

In the macho world, men are expected to demonstrate their virility, regardless of their marital status. Sexual conquests elicit other men's admiration. These conquests are a sign of a man's strength, importance, and cunning. In the novel's first chapter, "Antojos," the narrative informs us of the "Whore hour." In this passage, a male cousin brags to Yolanda about how a man of the upper class will visit his mistress on the "way home to his wife" (7). This constitutes a societal practice, the islanders' version of "Happy Hour." But sexual conquests are not only limited to Latin American men. Rudy, of "The Rudy Elmenhurst Story," proves persistent in his efforts to persuade Yolanda to have sex with him. He even shows up at her apartment five years after she had rejected him to attempt once again to seduce her. The reader should also consider Victor, the CIA agent. When he is first introduced in the narrative he is in a house of prostitution, where he is obviously a regular customer. His character reveals how macho behavior crosses cultural, ethnic, and geographical boundaries.

Inherent in the codes governing macho behavior is the need among men to cover up for each other's sexual indiscretions. Manuel, Fifi's island boyfriend, is the illegitimate son of Orlando, a paternal uncle of the García sisters. Orlando has fathered many children out of wedlock with a woman of modest economic means who lives in the countryside. His wife knows nothing about his other life. However, when Manuel starts appearing around the family compound, another uncle, Ignacio, stands up to claim Manuel as his illegitimate son. Ignacio, however, has his own motives for becoming the fall guy. He does this to divert attention from the speculation that he may be a homosexual, a rumor that follows him because he is middle-aged and unmarried. Being gay is unacceptable in the macho world. Thus, the two brothers benefit by covering for one another. As machos, they conspire to watch one another's backs.

Machismo is also charged with double standards. While the men are expected, even urged, to experiment sexually beginning at a young age, the women in their families are expected to be pure, virginal. In "A Regular Revolution," Mundín, a legitimate cousin of the girls, is experienced in sexual conquests. He is in cahoots with Manuel as the latter's relationship with Fifi intensifies. However, Mundín will not hear of his sister Lucinda being anything but chaste. Mundín's attitude reflects the double standards inherent in machismo. In fact, the narrative states that he is two different people—thus he becomes the embodiment of the double standard. While attending college in the United States he professes to have liberal, pro-feminist views. However, once he returns to the island, he reverts to being macho. His beliefs vary according to the culture he is living in, not out of conviction, but out of what serves him best as a man.

Strongly embedded in the notion of machismo is the concept of honor. The respect, esteem, reputation, and dignity of a man hinges in large part on what he and others think about his honorability. Therefore, a man's self-concept, in patriarchal society, is intimately linked to this notion. Honor is manifested in many ways. Among them is the man's ability to protect the "virtue" or "purity" of the women in his family. This list of women includes one's mother, wife, sisters, and, in particular, daughters. We have already mentioned how Mundín is concerned with Lucinda's relationships with other men. It is perfectly acceptable for him to have a sexual life, but not for his sister. In the García family, Carlos, the father, constantly watches for threats to his daughters' purity. As a warning to the daughters, the father once stated: "I don't want loose women in the family" (28). When he reads Otto's love letters to Sofía, he becomes incensed to learn that they had been intimate. He is concerned because his youngest daughter has been "dragging (his) good name through the dirt" (30). In his eyes, Sofía's behavior categorizes her as a "whore" (30). She has lost her purity, and thus he risks losing the respect and the esteem he enjoys in society.

Carlos, however, is not the only one in the García family who subscribes to this notion of honor as revolving around a woman's chastity. Laura, the mother, also views the concept of honor as being dependent upon a woman's virtue. In the chapter "A Regular Revolution," the mother is surprised to discover that her daughters had marijuana in their possession because she has been, as the first-person plural narrative voice states, "worried sick about protecting our virginity since we'd hit puberty in this land of wild and loose Americans, and vice had entered through an unguarded orifice at the other end" (114). As the reader can observe, the mother also subscribes to the equation of virginity as honor, which is so closely associated with machismo. Her belief that a woman must remain a virgin until marriage demonstrates how effective Latin American culture has been in teaching women to comport themselves in ways that, although considerably restricting their freedoms, benefit men almost exclusively. Her watchfulness over her daughters protects Carlos's honor. After all, the most assured way for a man to protect his patrimony is by restricting the entry of other males into his territory.

Another feature of the concept of honor is based on a man's financial prowess. This is mostly a matter of showmanship. A man must demonstrate his ability to pay his own way as well as to pay for others. This is most evident in the chapter "Floor Show." In this instance, Carlos feels less of a man because the Fannings intend to pay for everyone's night out. Carlos has yet to establish himself economically in his new country, so he has little choice but to accept the invitation. This hurts his macho pride. Laura offers consolation by reminding him that when the Fannings were on the island they treated the American couple royally. This reminder, however, offers the family patriarch little solace. As the narrative later informs the reader, on the island the men fight for the honor of paying for dinner. In fact, Carlos's honor is put into question once again toward the end of the chapter when Sandi, acting against her mother's stern warning, places the Fannings in a position to make a gift of the Spanish Barbie dolls. Carlos insists on paying for each of his daughters to have a doll, even though this was not within his means at the time. To make the affront to his honor worse, it is Mrs. Fanning—a free woman in comparison to Laura—who forces Carlos to let the girls accept the gifts. As a Latin American, he has been obliged to swallow his macho pride in this, his new country, which is something that would have never happened in his homeland.

In *How the García Girls Lost Their Accents*, though, men do get to exert, or to try to exert, their power over women. This is one of the novel's unquestionable features. The collective voice of the sisters in "A Regular Revolution" is acutely aware of the unfair advantage men have over women. In that chapter the sisters overtly condemn machismo when they describe their cousin Mundín as having a "myopic macho vision" (129). However, Alvarez is too intelligent of a writer to do this much thinking for her readers. The narrative expresses few opinions regarding machismo. The preponderance of the evidence indicates that the world she writes about, the culture that she presents to us, is out of balance. Latin American society, as portrayed in the novel, is overwhelmingly controlled by men. The reader cannot help but notice this even in the most superficial of readings. The Dominican-American author leaves it up to the reader to choose how to react to the sexism that is so pervasive in the book.

Alvarez does provide a sharp contrast between the conditions of women on the island—and by extension Latin America—and the condition of women in the United States. The narrative highlights how the options and freedoms that Latin American women do enjoy are restricted to a very few. In the chapter "Antojos," the reader encounters the case of Yolanda's cousin, Carmencita, who had learned English while studying at a boarding school in the United States for "two or three years." However, it also indicates that she did not continue her studies in this country because only "boys stay for college" (6). In "The Human Body" we find yet another case of a woman's lack of choices as represented in the character of Aunt Mimi. She is the most studious member of the family. Intellectually, she's the most gifted. But she was only allowed to attend an American college for two years because the family felt that too much education would spoil her for marriage. The irony is that she is still single at age twenty-eight, far beyond the age of marriage in Latin American society. Her time is, in the present of the narrative, solely devoted to gardening and reading books—an inordinate amount of books that serve little purpose other than to fill the days of a woman who is considered to be lonely and eccentric.

Women are also limited in other areas. In "Antojos," the family is scandalized by Yolanda's desire to travel throughout the country on her own. At her insistence she is allowed to do so, but only because her relatives acknowledge that she has become too Americanized. A woman who has lived her entire life on the island would never be allowed to undertake such a journey. Yolanda benefits here from her status as an outsider. In the Latin American society portrayed in *How the García Girls Lost Their Accents*, gender determines what an individual can and cannot do. Gender also determines what women can become. In "The Human Body," the mother, Laura, disapproves of the cowgirl outfit her mother gives Yolanda. She believes that it encourages the young girl's boyish behavior. A woman could never be a cowboy is the message conveyed to the young Yolanda. The mother argues that it is time for Yolanda to grow out of her tomboy phase and to begin to behave like "a young lady señorita" (228). In other words, Laura wants Yolanda to behave according to what Latin American culture has prescribed as appropriate for her gender, even at such an early age. Once again, the reader observes how women also enforce patriarchal codes of behavior.

Laura, however, is not alone in enforcing these codes. In "A Regular Revolution," the three sisters comment that they have given up on raising the consciousness of their Latin American relatives who are women with regard to their rights. They state that such an enterprise would "be like trying for cathedral ceilings in a tunnel" (121). They relate the specific incident of their Tía Flor who, when told by the sisters to protest for her rights, counters that she has a wonderful life: she is the queen of her house, her husband has to go to work every day, and she gets to sleep until noon. What else could be better, she argues. In her eyes, this is the way of life. She is comfortable with the limited role prescribed for her gender. Tía Flor represents the sentiments that the sisters, much to their frustration, find in the women of the island. The islanders have unquestioningly accepted the supremacy of men. A woman's role is that of wife, mother, and mistress of the house, nothing more.

The sisters, on the other hand, having become Americanized, or rather, having lost their accents, benefit from the greater privileges that women enjoy in the United States. The narrative asserts that their adoptive homeland represents little restrictions and more freedom of action for women when compared to the island (108–109). In fact, even Laura, who grew up on the island, is awakening to feminism by way of her Americanization. She demonstrates this by enrolling in college courses, and more significantly, when she decides to discipline Fifi herself after the marijuana incident. Traditionally, she would have left the punishment up to her husband.

The sisters, however, represent a woman's right to choose her own path in life. When visiting the island, the García sisters stand as infinitely more liberated than their female relatives. For instance, the Americanized women openly support birth control for women, a stance that shocks the islanders. Their support for women's rights is, in comparison, so revolutionary that they think of themselves as extremists. They, in a politically radical simile, mold themselves after the Argentine hero of the Cuban Revolution, Che Guevara, in their quest to liberate Fifi from the island's conservatism. In essence, Fifi's liberation is a metaphor for what they wish they could do for all the women of Latin America—to have them awaken and rebel against patriarchal society and machismo.

The sisters, though, cannot be portrayed as fervent militants for women's causes. Hardcore feminism is not something that any of them embrace. The world they come from, in fact, is far too complex for them to devote their energies fully to the struggle for women's rights. Yes, they are immensely freer than their Latin American counterparts. However, to a great extent, they are products of this very culture. Although they suffer because of men's dominance over women, the relationship they have with men is far from antagonistic. They have fought and struggled to be accepted as equals in American society. But this is as much a question of race and ethnicity as it is of gender. Their battles for acceptance and for their rights have been fought on two fronts.

When they take on patriarchal society, though, they do not always do so as full-fledged opponents. Carla, the eldest and most formally educated of the sisters, marries someone who is her equal and treats her as such. On the other hand, both Yolanda and Sandi have experienced severe setbacks in their romantic relationships, and they have both suffered breakdowns because of it. Still, at least Yolanda holds hopes of finding her ideal man. Fifi, who is the most contented, has accepted the role of wife and mother wholeheartedly. Yet no reader would question her determination and drive to choose what is best for her. After all, she, more than any of the other sisters, takes on the fight against patriarchy as represented by her father. Furthermore, she is the one who pursues Otto to a foreign country and proposes marriage to him. One can never question her strength. So, to Alvarez's credit, the sisters constitute a wide spectrum of feminist behaviors and attitudes.

Gender warfare is not what characterizes the relationships between men and women in *How the García Girls Lost Their Accents*. The relationships detailed within the pages of this novel are much more complex precisely because of the duality of the Garcías' cultural heritage. The sisters want the right to choose their own destinies. But at the same time they seek to have meaningful relationships with men. This means, to a great extent, catering to the male ego. Uncompromising feminism is not what defines them as characters. In fact, there is a brief, somewhat satirical statement regarding Yolanda that reads: "But the third daughter, who had become a feminist in the wake of her divorce . . ." (33). This comment suggests that only when deeply hurt does Yolanda turn to feminism and become an advocate for women's rights. But it is mostly a reaction to a failed relationship rather than a cause she embraces with full conviction. Her feminism, although heartfelt at that moment, is only a phase that she goes through until she is fully healed again and ready to embark on a new romance.

The highly ambivalent sentiments that the sisters have toward gender struggles, towards the male-dominated world they come from, is best summed up toward the end of the chapter "A Regular Revolution." The sisters triumph decidedly in their fight against patriarchy, machismo, and conservatism when they succeed in liberating Fifi from Manuel's grasp. They are now all free again. But because they created so much havoc in their efforts, Laura states that she will never send her daughters back to the island for they have proven to be too much trouble. To this, their Tía Carmen states that she would miss them terribly if they didn't come to visit every year. It is here where the sisters realize that not all is black and white in the struggle for women's rights. They are deeply moved by their aunt's affection, and unconditional love. At present they are liberated from the island's machismo. The door leading to freedom is wide open. They will never have to return to the repressive ways of their homeland. They can live out the rest of their lives in their much more liberated adoptive country. The narrative then states that in the way in which they are feeling, they are akin to the monkey experiment Carla had read about in college: the baby monkeys, their cage doors open, do not leave because they had been there for so long they don't seem to know how to take advantage of the opportunity to flee; they know of no other way of life. Besides, in spite of the machismo with which their culture is saturated, they know that within its boundaries, however imperfect that world may be, they are truly loved and safe.

4

In the Time of the Butterflies
(1994)

On November 25, 1960, henchmen of the Dominican ruler, Rafael Trujillo, murdered three sisters: Minerva, Patria, and María Teresa Mirabal. These women had dared to openly oppose the dictator's regime. The sisters, also known by their revolutionary code name, *Las Mariposas* (The Butterflies), had become symbols of resistance to Trujillo's rule. Their deaths stunned the Dominican people, and it marked the beginning of the end of Trujillo's dictatorship—the second longest one-person rule in the history of the continent. Rafael Leonidas Trujillo had ruthlessly governed the nation since 1930. He was gunned down by his own military in May of 1961, less than six months after the murder of the Butterflies. The elimination of the Mirabal sisters made it impossible for the dictator to continue his governance of the Dominican Republic. His assassination became the military's only option to guarantee its own survival. The Butterflies, through their deaths, had become national heroines, and their compatriots demanded justice. Their martyrdom also earned international recognition: the United Nations declared November 25, the date of their deaths, the International Day Against Violence Against Women.

In 1994, Algonquin Books of Chapel Hill published *In the Time of the Butterflies*. The Dominican-American's historical novel received overwhelming critical praise and it was nominated for the 1995 National Book Critics Circle Award. In "Chasing the Butterflies," which can be found in Julia Alvarez's collection of essays titled *Something to Declare*, the Dominican-American author writes about how the story of the Mirabal sisters had haunted her since the age of ten. In particular, it deeply affected her because of the ties between the Butterflies and Alvarez's family. Her father had been part of the same revolutionary underground as the Mirabal sisters, and his involvement in the plot to overthrow Trujillo had forced the Alvarez family to flee the Dominican Republic for the United States. While in the Dominican Republic researching a project on the Mirabal sisters, Alvarez met Noris, Patria's daughter, who in turn introduced her to Minou, Minerva's daughter. In 1992, six years after meeting the descendants of the Mirabal sisters, Alvarez met Dedé, the only surviving sister. As the Dominican-American writer describes it, after this meeting, she was inspired to undertake the task of portraying the lives of the Mirabal sisters in the form of a novel.

PLOT DEVELOPMENT AND STRUCTURE

In contrast to Alvarez's first novel, *In the Time of the Butterflies* has a straightforward, easily discernible plot. For the most part, Alvarez avoids experimentation with regard to plot and structure. The organization of incident and character is traditional. The Dominican-American writer recognizes that the story of the lives, and deaths, of the Mirabal sisters is powerful enough to sustain the reader's interest without resorting to unnecessary artifices. Alvarez develops the plot, with the exception of the beginning of each of Dedé's chapters, in a linear, chronological fashion. Her adherence to a traditional arrangement helps induce curiosity and suspense in the reader. The plot and structure of *In the Time of the Butterflies* are well constructed. As a consequence the readers feel that Alvarez is always in control of the story. Every event that Alvarez narrates leads to the next logical event, and this ultimately leads to a satisfying climax in which the reader's questions are answered.

The plot is fairly simple. An interview woman, a Dominican-American, arrives at Dedé's house in search of information regarding the lives of the Mirabal sisters. The woman, Alvarez's alter-ego, wants to write their story for an American audience. The *gringa dominicana*'s interest in the Butterflies, and in particular her interest in the surviving sister, triggers Dedé's memories. Dedé's thoughts travel back to the moment that her mind has fixed as "zero" (7). Thus, through Dedé's recollections, the reader learns the tale of *Las Mariposas*.

The narrative tells of the girls' family life, their schooling, their loves, hopes, ambitions, and dreams; but more importantly, it focuses on their gradual yet steady political awakening. As the Mirabal sisters mature, they become indignant toward the political injustices of their nation. Eventually they commit themselves to changing Dominican society—in essence, they become revolutionaries. At the onset, in the sisters' minds, the idea of a revolution seems glamorous, exciting, and even sexy. However, after Minerva slaps the Dominican dictator at the Discovery Day Dance, the situation becomes dangerous. Still, the sisters, with the exception of Dedé, continue to plot Rafael Trujillo's overthrow. After the plot fails, Minerva, María Teresa, and other family members are imprisoned and tortured. The government confiscates their property. In the process, however, the Mirabals become powerful symbols of resistance. The Dominican people look upon them as examples of courage and determination. The people's admiration, though, turns them into political targets. The dictator wishes aloud for the elimination of this "problem," and one of Trujillo's henchmen, eager to please his leader, complies. *Las Mariposas* are murdered, but their deaths mark the beginning of their legacy—a legacy that survives to this day, as evidenced in the epilogue, the postscript, and most notably in the very existence of *In the Time of the Butterflies*.

The structure of the novel reflects the straightforwardness of the plot. The formal structure of a novel consists of its parts, chapters, and their interdependent balance. *In the Time of the Butterflies* is divided into three parts, an epilogue, and a postscript. The three parts reflect the chronological progression of the novel: Part I narrates events from 1938–1946; Part II from 1948–1959; and Part III covers the tragic events of 1960. The perspective of each Mirabal sister is represented once in each section. The chapters narrated from Dedé's point of view initiate each part. Dedé's chapters bring the reader to 1994, the present of the narrative. Then through her recollections, the reader travels back into the past. Initiating each section in the present serves to highlight the legacy of the Butterflies, as well as Dedé's role as the oracle.

Part I of *In the Time of the Butterflies* focuses on the childhood and adolescence of the Mirabal sisters. In this section, Alvarez develops her main characters. Part I covers their family life, their schooling, Patria's marriage, and the loss of her first child. More importantly, however, it explores the political awakening of each of the sisters. Their eyes are opened, through various events, to the cruelty and injustices of Rafael

Trujillo's dictatorship. Each sister, on her own, but with Minerva as catalyst, comes to the painful awareness that Dominicans live in terror of their own government.

Part II carries the greater structural weight concerning the Butterflies' activities in opposition to the rule of Rafael Trujillo. In addition, this section deals with the discovery that their father, Enrique Mirabal, has another family that also consists of four daughters. This discovery leads the Mirabal women to question everything they hold sacred. Even Dedé, the most cautious and conservative of the sisters, begins to question her world. Through Virgilio Morales, better known as Lío (an interlanguage word-play as *lío* in Spanish also means a mess, a mix-up, a complication, or a jam), Minerva arrives at the realization that it is necessary to oppose Trujillo's reign by working with others in an organized fashion. Lío, a physician who also teaches in the university, has been labeled a communist by Trujillo's government. Therefore, his movements are closely monitored. His appearance in the novel also helps to introduce the presence and ideas of Fidel Castro, then a young and relatively unknown attorney struggling against the dictatorship of Fulgencio Batista. Castro's name, deeds, and ideas were just beginning to spread throughout the Caribbean. Castro's political views profoundly influence the sisters, as later they will influence millions of other Latin Americans.

By the time that Minerva catches Trujillo's eye, she has already developed highly revolutionary notions—and her sisters are following suit. After Minerva slaps the dictator, members of Trujillo's secret police discover Lío's letters in the purse she had inadvertently left behind. Her affiliation with a known "communist" places her on Trujillo's blacklist. Her father is imprisoned and she is brought in for questioning. The Dominican dictator, however, gives Minerva one more opportunity to redeem herself by sharing his bed. She adamantly refuses his offer. Minerva's refusal, however, condemn her and her family to exist in permanent opposition to Trujillo's regime. After her father's death, Minerva marries Manolo, another young attorney with revolutionary ideas—the Dominican equivalent to Fidel Castro.

Also in Part II of *In the Time of the Butterflies*, through Patria, the reader learns how the Catholic Church, after decades of collaborating with Trujillo, has now turned against him. After the attack Patria witnesses during her religious retreat, three of the four Mirabal sisters are full-blown revolutionaries. This concludes Part II.

After the failure of the plot to overthrow Trujillo, Part III centers on the Mirabals' plight. More tragically, this section narrates their last days.

It is here that the reader experiences Dedé's growth as a character. As her sisters suffer as a result of their persecution, Dedé emerges as the family anchor, and ultimately as the one who will be obliged to carry on her sisters' legacy. The plot reaches its climax in the novel's final chapter. As the sisters' situation becomes highly precarious, the narrative appears to accelerate, keeping the reader in suspense while maintaining alive the hope that somehow the Butterflies can, this time, elude their fate. Chapter 12, told from Minerva's point of view, concludes with the sisters' dilemma of whether or not to travel over the mountain pass. As night approaches, from the store where they last stopped to purchase refreshments, Minerva repeatedly tries to call home, but the line is busy. This device leaves the connection open for the story to continue beyond their deaths. There is a playful tone in the chapter's final segment. However, the reader is painfully aware that the fate of the Butterflies is sealed: the sisters will not reach the other side of the mountain. The light-heartedness magnifies the tragedy of their deaths and it brings the third section to a close.

The Epilogue represents the novel's dénouement, or the narration of the events that follow the plot's major climax. The Epilogue at last allows Dedé to tell her story from the first-person point of view. The sister who survived recalls how she received the news of her sisters' deaths, as well as how, through the information she received from partial witnesses, she was able to reconstruct their last living moments. In addition, the Epilogue updates the reader on the fates of other protagonists of the story, including Trujillo. It also tells of the descendants of the Butterflies. At the Epilogue's conclusion, Dedé is unveiled as the medium, the oracle through which the ghosts of the Mirabal family have told their stories.

The Postscript constitutes a brief yet fascinating look into the creation of *In the Time of the Butterflies*. In this section, Alvarez notes her father's close connection with the revolutionary underground, a connection that forced the Alvarez family to flee to the United States as political exiles. The Dominican-American writer also describes her personal fascination with the story of *Las Mariposas*. In her mind—the mind of a novelist— as she considered writing the tale of the Dominican heroines, the characters began to take control of the story. Thus, Alvarez affirms, what the reader encounters in her novel are neither the Mirabals of fact nor of legend—for their legendary status has removed their humanity. The Mirabals portrayed are the Mirabals of Alvarez's creation. The Postscript also informs the reader of how the Mirabals' sacrifice earned worldwide recognition in the form of the commemoration of the date of their deaths.

To conclude her Postscript, Alvarez states her intent behind the writing of the novel: to deepen "North Americans' understanding of the nightmare" that Dominicans have endured and of the heavy losses they have suffered (324).

CHARACTER DEVELOPMENT

Julia Alvarez develops well-rounded characters in her second novel. The Mirabal sisters possess very distinct personalities. Each of the Butterflies represents a different facet of the political awakening of Dominicans to the evils of Rafael Trujillo's dictatorship, as well as to their need to foment a revolution. Alvarez skillfully achieves characterization, or the development of a character, by way of the traits with which she has endowed each leading character, and the manner in which they put these traits to work. The Dominican-American writer ably portrays all four sides of each Mirabal sister: their general, physical, personal, and emotional nature. Alvarez combines insight and richness in order to achieve good characterization. The insight in characterization comes from the Dominican-American's knowledge of what her leading characters want from life.

Without a doubt, Minerva Mirabal emerges as the novel's strongest character. This is a reflection of Dominican history—a history that considers her the intellect and the heart behind the Butterflies' opposition to Trujillo. Minerva, above all things, constitutes the embodiment of the determination, persistence, and strength necessary for revolutions to succeed. From the moment readers meet Minerva, we are aware of these aspects of her characterization.

Minerva's political awakening begins in the section of Chapter Two titled "Complications." In the narrative, "Complications," a nun's euphemism for menstruation, also stands as a metaphor for Minerva's birth as a political being. While attending school, a classmate, Sinita, opens Minerva's eyes to the evils of Rafael Trujillo's rule. After Sinita relates "Trujillo's secret," Minerva's "complications" begin. The onset of Minerva's first menstrual cycle is superimposed on her recent awareness of the injustices rampant in her nation. Combined, they represent a stunning metaphor for her loss of innocence.

Later in the novel, another character, Lío, contributes substantially to Minerva's political maturation. In fact, the narrative credits him with shaping her political ideology (86). Lío, whose name in Spanish literally renders him another "complication," introduces Minerva to new doctrines as well as to Latin America's burgeoning rebellions, particularly the incipient Cuban Revolution. These examples inspire her to begin acting in opposition to Trujillo's regime. Minerva's association with Lío, in addition to earning her a spot on the dictator's blacklist, teaches her to think independently, to become a stalwart of the growing underground that will challenge the strongman's reign. Eventually, her energy and her commitment to the cause of freedom act as a vortex, drawing all of the sisters in.

While all the Mirabal sisters, at one time or another, exhibit leadership traits, none does so more than Minerva. Her leadership skills are most evident during her imprisonment. While in confinement, Minerva leads the political prisoners in singing the Dominican national anthem, an ironic manifestation of their continued rebellion. She organizes classes and open discussions for her cellmates. She conducts these events not only for political prisoners, but for common criminals as well. Her educational endeavors bring to mind Fidel Castro, who during his imprisonment on the Isle of Pines did the same. Minerva also organizes the "crucifix plot." When prison officials order Minerva to desist, her brave resistance earns María Teresa's admiration. When the pressures of prison life break Mate, it is Minerva who supplies her with the strength to endure. Without a doubt, throughout *In the Time of the Butterflies*, Minerva stands as the clear leader.

Strong-willed and independent, Minerva's opposition to other characters often defines her. An intense sibling rivalry characterizes her relationship with Dedé. From childhood they are opposites. Dedé is a meticulous, detailed individual. On the other hand, Minerva is a dreamer, an individual who dares to live life in broad, adventurous strokes. Their rivalry comes to a climax when Lío appears on the scene. Both sisters are attracted to the charismatic physician. Although Dedé is engaged to her future husband, Jaimito, she is interested in the possibility of a relationship with Lío. However, Minerva finds herself strongly drawn to Lío's political views and, more importantly, she is unattached. Thus, she develops the closer bonds with him, making Dedé jealous. From this moment on, they become somewhat estranged from one another. Nevertheless, the ties of sisterhood are too strong to be severed. When Dedé's marriage is at its most troublesome, Minerva supports her and excuses her sister from participating in the revolutionary underground. Minerva, as well as Manolo, assure Dedé that indeed she is brave and that her personal battle is as important as their revolutionary

struggle. By the same token, Dedé demonstrates on more than one occasion that she is willing to die for her younger sister.

Certainly, Minerva's opposition to Rafael Trujillo is what most sharply
defines her. Since adolescence she abhors the dictator. Minerva and her
school friends stage a play before the dictator and his son, Ramfis. The
drama is intended as a veiled criticism of the regime. However, Sinita,
acting on her own, decides to make the criticism overt. In this instance,
Minerva quickly steps in to save the day by initiating a chorus of cheers
for Trujillo. A few years later, while still attending school, she becomes
involved in clandestine political meetings in which radical solutions to
her country's problems are discussed. After graduation she meets Lío,
and she becomes cognizant of the need to help organize the struggle
against Trujillo. However, it is not until the Discovery Day Dance that
Minerva directly confronts the despot. The ensuing slap marks the beginning of a highly personal antagonism—an antagonism that eventually
proves fatal for both of them. When Minerva meets the dictator once
again, to request her father's release from prison, she rolls the die against
the despot: at stake, whether Minerva attends college or whether he beds
her. The contest of wills fittingly ends in a tie. Their final confrontation
is left to another time. The entire tragedy that constitutes the foundation
of the novel arises from the tension caused by Minerva's opposition to
Rafael Trujillo.

Although Minerva represents the persistent, determined, and strong
revolutionary, even she has her limits. During her imprisonment, Minerva begins to exhibit her vulnerability. Throughout her incarceration,
Minerva remains a pillar of strength. However, toward the end of their
time in prison, Mate becomes concerned that Minerva is reaching her
breaking point. The leader of the Butterflies begins to behave somewhat
erratically. After Minerva's release, she suffers from sensory overload.
The sounds of freedom disturb her. She has become an agoraphobic, a
recluse who barely leaves her room. Ironically, while strong in prison,
once free Minerva feels weak. She now wants an ordinary life. She finds
pleasure in many of the little things she took for granted prior to prison,
such as the color of pinto beans. Minerva wants to touch, taste, and
experience everything anew. Although initially the memories of prison
are painful, the passage of time begins to heal them. At the end of her
life, Minerva is wiser with regard to her limitations. Although she never
fully regains her former, irresolute self, she remains, in all of her glorious
stubbornness, opposed to Rafael Trujillo's dictatorship.

Minerva's brave stand against the Dominican despot makes her a heroine in the eyes of her compatriots. After her release from prison, whenever Minerva ventures out of the house, the people treat her as a woman of extraordinary courage. Although Minerva plays the role graciously, she accepts it with reluctance. Even during mass, the Catholic Church, represented by Father Gabriel, expresses its admiration for her. Dr. Viñas, the underground's new leader, tells Minerva that she, more than anyone else in the country, needs to keep her hopes up. He tells her that she needs to continue believing that things will change because the Dominican people see in her a sterling example of how to resist Trujillo. As their role model, Minerva cannot show her vulnerability, only her resolve and her strength. Without a doubt, Minerva Mirabal constitutes one of Julia Alvarez's most remarkable characters.

In comparison to Minerva's, Patria's character development appears simple and straightforward. This appearance, however, is misleading. The eldest of the Mirabal sisters represents an important sector of Latin American revolutionaries: those who, because of their religious faith, commit themselves to improve the world. Patria's religiosity is unquestionably her most salient character trait. In the novel's first chapter, Dedé bristles when the interview woman mentions Patria's fixation on religion. The surviving sister, like Julia Alvarez, does not want Patria to be remembered as having been one-dimensional. Nevertheless, she is best defined vis-à-vis her religious faith. From the moment in which the narrative first introduces Patria, she is seen as not of this earth. The mother states that at first she was afraid that Patria wouldn't be around for long, that her eldest daughter was "already the way we (are) to become" (45). In other words, that Patria belongs more of the spiritual realm than to the physical. The nuns in the school take early notice of Patria's piety. They invite her to join their order. Thus, from the onset, the young girl's religiosity is evident to all.

Patria, however, as an adolescent, experiences the all-too-human conflict between the spirit and the flesh. She is torn between her calling toward a religious life at the service of the Catholic Church and the desires of her body. Her dilemma is resolved when she meets her future husband, Pedro. At that moment, the needs of the spirit and the flesh merge. Meeting Pedro constitutes, in itself, a religious experience. It takes place during Easter week, on Holy Thursday, as Patria helps reenact when Jesus washed the feet of his apostles. She realizes at that very moment that although she is destined to marry, she need not forsake her God or her Church.

Indeed, questions of faith and of service characterize Patria's adulthood. When Patria loses what would have been her third-born child, she experiences a crisis of faith. Wracked by pain, and tormented by her loss, she exhumes the body of her stillborn child. In her grief-stricken mind, among other things, the promise of the resurrection has not been fulfilled. Faced with the decomposition of the flesh, Patria is left to question everything she has ever held sacred. In the meantime, the eldest of the Mirabal sisters becomes concerned over Minerva's growing involvement in politics. Slowly, though, Patria becomes aware that grave injustices plague her nation. Nevertheless, in Patria's mind, politics and religion are not natural bedfellows. Thus, she is left, painfully alone, to reflect on her loss of faith. The five Mirabal women, each with a different petition in mind, embark on a pilgrimage to Higüey, where reportedly the *Virgencita* was sighted. Patria's petition, of course, is to ask the Virgin Mary to restore her faith. At the conclusion of their pilgrimage, in the chapel where a hopeful populace has gathered to honor the *Virgencita*, Patria hears a voice that tells her that the spirit of Mary rests not in the image before her, but rather all around her, in the people and their suffering.

Patria begins to understand that religion and politics do intersect, particularly in times of grave injustices. She becomes more sympathetic to Minerva's involvement in the underground, although she herself is not ready to join. While Patria attends a spiritual retreat in search of a Christian answer to her nation's ills, she experiences a profound conversion when a young rebel is killed before her eyes. Like Moses, she descends from the mountain retreat a changed person (162). In addition to being a committed Christian, Patria has now also become a full-blown revolutionary. Her religious and political views have merged. Her faith now dictates that her mission is to help change the unjust society in which Dominicans live.

The strength of her newfound convictions, however, is severely tested. The underground's plot to overthrow Trujillo fails. As a consequence, her husband and son are among the imprisoned. During her son's arrest, Patria begs the guards to take her instead, ". . . for the love of God" (195). This will become an often-repeated leitmotif, as Patria offers herself to God in exchange for her son's life. At this point in the narrative, Alvarez describes Patria's suffering by way of biblical metaphors. The eldest of the Mirabal sisters resurrects "on the third day" from her depression; and she prays for everyone's resurrection. The narrative also describes Patria's suffering as a cross and a crown of thorns. Thus, what Patria has to endure becomes Christlike.

Patria's behavior, guided by her faith, makes her generous in deed and in spirit. She is the most selfless of the Mirabal sisters. More than any of the others, she is the peacemaker. Patria is always willing to seek a compromise with her opponents. As her mother states, "Patria's sweetness could move mountains, and monsters" (272). In addition, she gives of herself patiently, and totally, for the well-being of others. Above all, however, she is the consummate wife and mother. Patria is gentle in her pursuit of Pedrito after they first meet. The narrative employs an image that brings to mind Saint Francis: Patria tries to coax Pedrito, like a wild animal, to eat out of her hand. Later, in a reference to Saint Peter, Patria builds the foundation of her house on a rock (Pedro = Peter = rock). She sets aside her own needs, her personal growth, in order to become the perfect wife and mother. Patria criticizes her sisters—very mildly— for building their houses on sand and calling the slipping and sliding of their shoddy foundations an adventure. However, as a result of her devotion to her family, after laboring for years on this project, she loses her sense of self. Perhaps that is why Patria demonstrates a feminist streak when she expresses that she wants her daughter, Noris, to grow up to be independent. Patria hopes that her daughter will never have to rely on a man to support her. The eldest of the Mirabal sisters is also highly protective of Nelson, her son. Indeed, Patria's maternal instincts are what turn her into a committed revolutionary when the face of the boy killed during the retreat becomes deeply etched into her soul. She adopts him as hers, and she makes the solemn promise that his death will not be in vain.

From her conversion on, Patria demonstrates that she also can be a leader. At first, Patria offers a secluded area of her farm for the underground to meet. She, however, remains at the margin of their revolutionary activities. But after she returns from the mountain retreat, in a display of leadership, she invites the rebels inside the house, thus joining the underground herself. By offering her home as refuge, she becomes the mother of the underground, its matriarch. After the plot to overthrow Trujillo fails, as the government lays siege to the Mirabal sisters, Patria becomes the family's spiritual leader. After Minerva and María Teresa are released from prison, Patria leads them every night in praying the rosary. Even Minerva, who normally shuns religion, returns to Catholicism through Patria. Undisputedly, the eldest of the Mirabal sisters constitutes the spiritual center of *In the Time of the Butterflies*.

If Minerva represents the intellectual side, and Patria the spiritual side of *Las Mariposas*, then María Teresa, or Mate, embodies their romantic side. Many individuals join a revolution because it fulfills certain romantic expectations. One can change the world, making it better for everyone else, and in the process have a great adventure. This adventure can include finding one's true love. Mate is one of these romantics. Alvarez develops María Teresa primarily through diary entries. Initially, these brim with innocence. They constitute a child's view of the world. When the readers first meet María Teresa, her religious nature, like Patria's, is evident. However, unlike the eldest of her sisters, Mate does not hear the calling to join the nunnery. In fact, from an early age she is curious about sexuality. Nevertheless, Mate remains very innocent. When she learns about sex, from Minerva's explanations as well as from her own observations of animal life on the family farm, the youngest of the Mirabal sisters expresses her hope that by the time she is married a new method of reproduction will be found.

Politically, Mate is the most naïve of the sisters. While still attending school, Minerva makes political comments that are out of Mate's grasp. Later, Minerva leaves school without permission to attend clandestine political meetings. Mate covers for her. Mate's curiosity about Minerva's statements and nightly activities constitute the beginning of her political awakening. The questions she asks Minerva, however, reveal her innocence (38–39). At the conclusion of Chapter Three, the first chapter told from María Teresa's point of view, she buries her diary out of fear that her writings will incriminate her and Minerva if Trujillo's police should find them. This burial, superimposed on the funeral of Patria's child, represents the death of Mate's innocence.

Once María Teresa's profound interest in boys begins, so does her full political awakening. In fact, in her diary entries, boys and politics are often superimposed upon one another. Mate's greatest ambition as a child, adolescent, and later as a young adult, is to find her true love. To this desire, Minerva counters that rather than wasting her time thinking about this, Mate would be better off developing her mind. Still, the youngest of the Mirabal sisters remains a hopeless romantic. A leitmotif of the diary entries are María Teresa's marriage scenarios: "¿Beto and Mate?," or "¿Mate and Raúl?," or "Mate and Justico," or "Mate and Armando," etc. Thus, the reader finds that Mate's character is in great part driven by her attraction to men. Even while Mate attends the university, her major coincides with her romantic nature. She chooses Philosophy and Letters, which Minerva argues is for women whose only goal is to find a husband.

It should not surprise the reader, then, that María Teresa's love for a man is the catalyst for her full political awakening. While staying for a brief period with Minerva and Manolo, Mate falls in love with a member of the underground who in the middle of the night delivers a mysterious box. This is also the first time that she hears the code name *Mariposa*. Because of the romantic potential of the underground, Mate becomes a revolutionary. Although María Teresa participates fully in the movement, she admits that she joined because of her attraction to Leandro Guzmán, code name "Palomino." Mate writes in her diary: "I admit that for me love goes deeper than the struggle" (147). Nevertheless, loyal and romantic, her devotion to the cause can never be questioned.

Perhaps Mate's emotional, volatile side is what makes her such an interesting character. When writing about the death of Patria's child, Mate expresses succinctly the essence of her characterization: "I better stop until I get over my emotions" (42). In fact, another diary entry states that her mother considers Mate the moodiest of the sisters, and the youngest of the family fully concurs with this assessment. When Mate is elected Miss University, the disappearance and presumed murder of Professor Galíndez in New York so affects her that she considers refusing the honor. Minerva, however, convinces her that it is imperative that she accept the only democratically elected post in the nation. Mate, thus, sets her feelings aside and decides to help keep the democratic process alive for the sake of her compatriots.

Without a doubt, María Teresa is the character that grows most throughout the course of the novel. The reader experiences her entire life: beginning with the innocence of childhood, through adolescence, and young adulthood. We witness her continued development when she later becomes wife, mother, and revolutionary. Sadly, Mate matures most during her imprisonment. Although the prison experience initially overwhelms her, with time, as her suffering increases, so does her strength. Not surprisingly, her strength is compassionate. Rather than hating those who have hurt her, she learns to love them. Also, María Teresa becomes independent in prison. She develops a mind of her own, no longer following in Minerva's footsteps or unquestioningly accepting her directions. For instance, after Mate's torture, Minerva asks for details about what took place. Mate, however, remains stubbornly silent on the issue. She refuses to become a subject of protest. She wants to keep the matter private. She refuses to tell anyone what took place, even though she could exonerate Leandro, her husband, who has been accused of betraying the cause. Also while in prison, Mate becomes aware of the primary difference between Minerva and herself: for the older sister revolution has become a habit, a habit that she cannot break. Mate, on the other hand, has decided that after her release from prison she will remain at the margins, discontinuing her involvement in the underground.

Like the other Butterflies, Mate demonstrates that she too possesses leadership qualities. When Minerva is placed in solitary confinement, the youngest sister assumes the role of discussion leader. María Teresa conducts perhaps the most meaningful session of all. She and her cellmates discuss how important it is for women to develop strong bonds among themselves, regardless of education and socio-economic status. The participants conclude that residing in these bonds is the possibility of authentic social change. In fact, it is through Mate's prison diary that Alvarez most closely explores women's issues. Mate proves to be the most enlightened, yet compassionate, feminist among the Mirabal sisters.

At the other end of the spectrum, Dedé represents the pragmatic approach toward a revolution. For the most part, only idealists and romantics risk their lives in such dangerous enterprises. The gap between pragmatists and the others can be observed when, one night, as Dedé is engaged in conversation with Lío about changing Dominican society, she asks him where he gets his courage. He replies that it is not a matter of courage, but rather, of common sense. To his answer, Dedé reflects: "Common sense? Sitting around dreaming while the secret police hunted you down!" (77). This statement sums up Dedé's perspective on openly opposing Trujillo. Being practical, better suited to manage a store's inventory or solve math problems, the surviving sister sees no common sense in Lío's schemes. When Mate, brimming with enthusiasm, invites her to join the underground, Dedé is shocked both at the notion and the tone of the proposal: "As if they were inviting her to join a goddamn volleyball team!" (178). However, Dedé is in fact attracted to the idea of joining. The invitation tempts her. She also understands the need to remove Trujillo from power. Thus, when she refuses, she thinks of herself as a coward. Nevertheless, what prevails is her practical side. Dedé weighs the benefits against the risks and concludes that becoming involved in the enterprise is not worth it. One can say that history proves her correct. In fact, while in prison, Mate wishes that she had taken the same path as her more conservative sister (240). By the end of the novel, at least once, each of the Butterflies wished they had more of Dedé's "common sense."

The sister who survived best sums up the essence of Dedé's characterization (5). "(W)hy are you the one who survived?" is a question often asked, and it is one that greatly troubles her (5). Arguably, survival has been the most difficult of fates. Dedé carries the enormous burden of the past on her shoulders. *Las Mariposas* have become icons of the Dominican people. In search of some relief, she tries to think only of the family's happy moments. But invariably she gets caught up in the sadness of the entire story. Her husband's statement best sums her destiny: "This is your martydom, Dedé, to be alive without them" (308). In the present of the narrative, particularly in the epilogue, Dedé wonders how she made it through the pain. During the all-too-brief periods that her nation has enjoyed democracy, she feels that her sisters did not die in vain. However, Dedé also experiences great disillusionment whenever her country reverts to authoritarian rule. In these instances, she closes herself off to the world. As the reader can see, there is great pain in being the survivor.

In the novel, Dedé's primary function is to serve as the medium, the oracle of her sisters' legacy. In the present of the narrative, 1994, thirty-four years have passed since the deaths of *Las Mariposas*. By now Dedé is weary of visitors seeking information on her martyred sisters. The visits have become formulaic: glasses of lemonade made with lemons from the tree Patria planted, a quick tour of the house, a brief presentation, followed by a question-and-answer period. She agrees to receive the *gringa dominicana*, but she lies about a later commitment so that she can be rid early of the intruder. In short, when the reader meets Dedé, the burden of being the oracle has her exhausted.

Dedé's destiny as the Mirabals' standard-bearer, however, is inescapable. After her sisters' death, the Dominican people make her the depository of their own stories, for they too feel that they have played a part in the saga of *Las Mariposas*. Soon, the surviving sister has enough fragments of the puzzle to piece together the lives, and deaths, of her sisters. Ultimately, Dedé becomes the spokesperson for their legacy when, in the darkest hour of the Dominican people's struggle for democracy, she realizes that she needs to tell the story of her sisters. She hopes that through the tale of the Butterflies' sacrifice, the people of the Dominican Republic can come to terms with their personal losses. Thus Dedé, in a magnificent act of generosity, locks herself forever into the role that tires her, the role of the oracle.

In part, Alvarez develops Dedé's character in opposition to Minerva. As discussed earlier, a fierce sibling rivalry characterizes their relationship. They compete against one another, and this competition is never more intense than during the chase for Lío's attention. In fact, in the present of the narrative, as Dedé begins to recall that period, she winces when she discovers that, even after many years, she continues to compete

with her dead sister over Lío (66). The climax of their rivalry over Lío
constitutes a secret that Dedé shares only with the reader. Under the
guise of protecting her sister, but also with more than a trace of jealousy,
Dedé burns the letters in which Lío asks Minerva to join him in the
Colombian embassy, where he seeks political asylum. Dedé lives with
the guilt that if she had given Minerva the letters perhaps everyone's
destiny would be different, happier: her sisters might still be alive.

Their intense competition over Lío, however, also leads to Dedé's political awakening. When Dedé's mother discovers that the newspapers
are calling Lío a "communist," the eyes of the surviving sister are opened
to the injustices of Trujillo's dictatorship (74). Knowing that Lío is an
enemy of the state excites Dedé. She becomes wrapped up in his relationship with Minerva. Consequently, Dedé begins to question her
world, to accept the need for change. She begins to listen, clandestinely,
to Fidel Castro's radio speeches. Still, although ideologically she stands
alongside her sisters, her pragmatism never allows her to join the rebellion.

In reality, what impedes Dedé from joining is her troubled marriage.
Her relationship with Jaimito consumes all of her energies. Although
while engaged to her future husband she caught a glimpse of his true
nature, it was not until after their wedding that he became obsessively
domineering. His possessiveness and control over Dedé squelches her
spirit. After several years of marriage, and three sons, Dedé begins to
consider leaving him. In the narrative, superimposed on her nostalgia
for Lío, is her desire to be independent. Dedé's practice of listening to
Fidel's speeches constitutes her own private rebellion against Jaimito.
However, when she mentions her intentions of leaving him, he threatens
to take her sons away. This threat is superimposed on the moment that
her sisters invite her to join the underground. At this point in Dedé's
life, her survival as a mother takes precedent over her desire to help
change her nation.

Although Dedé considers herself a coward, when the Mirabal family
faces its greatest trial she becomes their anchor, their pillar of strength.
After Minerva and Mate are arrested, she takes care of the children. Her
mission now becomes to hold the family together and to save her sisters.
Through Dedé's strength and determination, the power shifts in her marriage. Dedé gains greater control of the relationship. But at this point
saving her sisters is more important. Dedé becomes so strong that she
holds the usually resolute Patria in place. For instance, when Patria
breaks down, as she leads the family in praying the rosary, Dedé takes

over. In fact, Patria directly credits Dedé with bringing her out of the depths of depression. During the Mirabals' time of greatest need, Dedé comes to the forefront, and in doing so she assumes the role of leader.

Tragically, in the end, she fails in her mission to save the Butterflies. Nevertheless, in reality, the true test of her strength begins after their deaths. She, the sister who survived, now has a sadder and perhaps more difficult mission: to be the keeper of the flame. Dedé, for the remainder of her life, must keep the ideals of *Las Mariposas* alive. In the end, because of the manner in which Dedé fulfills her obligations, she proves to be the strongest of all.

POINT OF VIEW

A point of view is simply the position of the narrator in relation to her story (see full explanation in Chapter 3). In other words, it is the outlook from which events are related. The manner in which Alvarez employs the point of view in her second novel helps bring each of the sisters' characters, as well as their stories, to life. The reader can virtually hear the voices of the Butterflies as they share their individual journeys. The Dominican-American's choice of viewpoints gives the story of the martyred sisters an immediacy and poignancy that is bound to touch every reader.

In Alvarez's work each chapter is told from a different point of view. The beginning of the chapter clearly states, in lieu of a title, from whose vantage point the story is told. Throughout the novel Alvarez employs the first-person and the third-person limited viewpoints. The dead sisters, Minerva, Patria, and María Teresa tell their version of events using the first-person shifting vantage point. In other words, from chapter to chapter they take turns telling the story. Dedé's side of events, however, is told from the third-person limited point of view—with the exception of the Epilogue, which she narrates in the first-person.

Alvarez employs, however, several innovative devices that make these points of view more interesting. One device is the presence of the author's alter-ego, or fictional self—the interview woman who, like Alvarez herself, happens to be a *gringa dominicana* (that is, half American, half Dominican). This character spurs Dedé's memories. It is her visit with the surviving sister that sparks the beginning of the story. The interview woman, more American than Dominican, is, culturally speaking, somewhat out of place. Dedé finds the woman's biculturalism odd. The *gringa*

dominicana demonstrates a linguistic as well as a cultural awkwardness
in the island environment. The cultural differences between the women
are highlighted early in the narrative when Dedé worries that the inter-
viewer will not understand the directions to her house, as well as when
the foreigner requests a specific time for the meeting. Nevertheless, this
minor character becomes the catalyst for Dedé's point of view to grow
and mature until it blossoms fully in the Epilogue. The interview
woman's unique cultural outlook intrigues Dedé. The *gringa dominicana*,
unlike most people, actually wants to know more about the surviving
sister than about the martyred Dominican heroines. It is the *gringa dominicana* who best expresses the spirit of the narrative when, in response
to Dedé's question regarding what precisely she would like to know, the
interview woman answers: "Tell me all of it" (7). The *gringa dominicana*
begins her interview by asking Dedé to recall one happy moment in their
lives. Immediately, the point of view of the surviving sister travels back
to a moment in her memory that she has designated as "zero," to the
beginning of the story of the Mirabal sisters (7). Gradually, as the novel
progresses, Dedé fully accepts the interview woman into her confidence.
Ironically, Dedé's acceptance also marks the eventual disappearance of
this character. At this juncture the *gringa dominicana* begins to fade, she
becomes "a shadowy face slowly losing its features" (171). Dedé's voice,
her point of view, grows in strength until it does not need the prompting
of the interview woman to finish telling the story.

Alvarez employs another device in relation to Dedé's viewpoint: the
medium. The medium, a person with the power to communicate with
the dead, is a device that Alvarez uses in all of her novels. In the
Dominican-American's second novel, Fela is the medium. The Haitian
maid becomes possessed "by the spirits of the girls" (63). People travel
from all corners of the Dominican Republic to visit Fela in order to con-
verse with the martyred sisters. These pilgrims ask Patria to cure them
of illnesses, María Teresa to help them with love woes, and Minerva to
assist them with impossible causes. Even Minou converses with her
mother, Minerva, through Fela. However, as the narrative progresses
Dedé and Fela begin to merge: "She [Dedé] takes a deep breath, just the
way Minou describes Fela doing right before the sisters take over her
body and use her old woman's voice . . ." (63). When the interview
woman prompts Dedé to reach into her memories to retrieve the story
of her sisters, the process of her becoming the medium begins. In this
manner the medium becomes a metaphor for memory. By the conclusion
of *In the Time of the Butterflies*, Dedé has graduated from the role of me-

dium: she has become the oracle. The surviving sister has become the transmitter of the Butterflies' legacy, of their sacrifice, of their hopes for a just nation. In the Epilogue, the reader discovers that Dedé has been telling us the story all along. She has summoned the ghosts of her sisters and assumed their voices; and in telling their stories to the interview woman, she puts their spirits to rest.

Alvarez employs yet another device to make a character's viewpoint more interesting: she tells María Teresa's, or Mate's, story by way of a diary. Each of the entries is dated, giving the reader an exact point in time of events. The diary conveys a great amount of history—personal, familial, national, and international. Furthermore, through Mate's diary, we receive an intimate, thorough account of her prison experience. But the details never overwhelm the reader. The diary also includes various modes of writing: newspaper clippings, poetry, love notes, wedding invitations, songs, menus, and speeches. Most prominent among the entries are Mate's drawings and diagrams. These take the reader from the innocence of Mate's childhood (with her drawings of bathing suits, purses, shoes, and rings), to her dangerous involvement in the underground, as depicted by the sinister diagram that shows how to build a time bomb. In addition, some of the diagrams, such as the layouts of the prison and of Minerva and Manolo's home, save us from extended descriptions that would have bogged down the pace of the narrative. Through Mate's artwork we see the world as she saw it. The diary makes María Teresa's viewpoint the most intimate and open of all. On the surface, it also gives María Teresa's perspective the appearance of being lighthearted. This is deceptive. However, the diary eases the tension in what otherwise is a profoundly tragic story.

LITERARY DEVICE: FORESHADOWING

Foreshadowing constitutes the technique of arranging events and information within the narrative in such a way that later occurrences are prepared for, or suggested, beforehand. A well-constructed novel can hint at the beginning what the outcome may be. Thus, the conclusion will be contained in the beginning, and this provides the work with structural as well as thematic unity. Foreshadowing also builds suspense as well as the expectations of the reader. The narrative of *In the Time of the Butterflies* is replete with events and information that foreshadow the novel's outcome. Of course, this outcome is tragic. In foreshadowing the deaths of the Mirabal sisters, Alvarez prepares her readers for the heart-rending conclusion. For instance, the Dominican-American writer often employs the metaphor of the approaching storm to heighten the sense of impending doom. In addition, all of the sisters exhibit an acute aware-ness of their destinies. In an image that foreshadows the family's fate, the narrative, presented from Dedé's perspective, imagines someone finding the bodies of all the Mirabals in a ditch because of Minerva's outspokenness (10). An early entry of Mate's diary mentions how the "brave heroes who die for what is right" moves Minerva's soul (31). In Mate's recurring dream about coffins, she, in essence, anticipates her own death. Also, Patria repeatedly offers her life in exchange for the lives of her husband and son.

In the novel's concluding chapter, because Minerva cannot describe her own death, Alvarez intensifies her use of foreshadowing to prepare her readers for the final outcome. To begin with, the driver, Rufino, tells Dedé that they'll have to kill him first before he lets anything happen to the sisters. During their last night in the Mirabal residence, as the lights go out, Minerva imagines herself a ghost that wanders about the house. On their final trip to visit the men in prison, Minerva's thoughts fore-shadow their fall down the cliff. Also foreshadowed is the ambush near one of Trujillo's mansions at a site bearing three crosses. Other characters warn the sisters, more than once, not to cross the mountain pass. In the end, however, history proves inflexible. It has already determined their fates. Even a writer as gifted as Alvarez cannot save them: the murder of *Las Mariposas* is a foregone conclusion.

On the other hand, Dedé, throughout *In the Time of the Butterflies*, an-ticipates with dread that she'll be the lone survivor. From childhood she seems aware of her role as the sister who survives. Her father predicts that "she'll bury us all" (8). In several instances, Dedé thinks, or states, that she does not want to go on living without her sisters. In one instance she is very explicit. After Dedé angrily scolds her sisters because they stubbornly insist on visiting their husbands in prison, as they depart she runs after their vehicle, crying: "I don't want to have to live without you" (266).

Julia Alvarez, however, plants some leads that in the end do not fulfill the reader's expectations. When the family discovers that the presumably innocent María Teresa is a full-fledged member of the underground, she asks Patria to take care of her children should anything happen. Thus Patria is foreshadowed as the one who will become the mother of the orphans. The husbands of the Butterflies anticipate their own deaths while in prison. Although Manolo eventually does die as a revolutionary, it does not occur under the circumstances he foreshadowed. Perhaps the most moving instance of a false lead can be found at the conclusion of the novel's final chapter. As *Las Mariposas* decide to cross the mountain pass, in spite of their misgivings, Minerva's mood is lighthearted. Like when they were children playing at night in their yard, they are a little bit afraid and a little bit excited by the risk they are taking. In making this comparison, Alvarez takes the reader back to one of their earliest memories. The reader wants the story to begin over again so that the Mirabal sisters can have another chance. This, however, is not the case. Ultimately, the worst fears are confirmed in the poignant epilogue. The false leads, however, keep the reader's hopes alive until the bitter end.

THEMATIC ISSUES

The predominant theme of *In the Time of the Butterflies* is the cruelty of Rafael Trujillo's dictatorship. His presence in the narrative overwhelms the reader. Before encountering the first word of the novel, the reader finds evidence of the despot's cruelty. On the inside flap of the cover are the names of victims of Trujillo's regime. In addition, Alvarez dedicates this book to Dedé, as well as to the memory of her martyred sisters and the chauffer who accompanied them on their final voyage. Thus, from the onset, even before the narrative begins, the formidable shadow of Trujillo's deeds looms sinisterly over the text.

What generates Alvarez's second novel is the opposition of the Mirabal sisters to Trujillo's dictatorship. In fact, to a large extent, this is what defines them as characters. As Dedé is giving the *gringa dominicana* a tour of the house, the surviving sister reflects on how their stand against the dictator has rendered them larger than life. Their mutual antagonism begins after Minerva slaps Trujillo at the Discovery Day Dance. Immediately afterwards, as the literal and metaphorical storm begins, the family hurriedly leaves the celebration. From this moment on, the Mirabals become targets. The slap, their rushed exit, and the incriminating letters discovered in Minerva's purse place the entire family on a collision course with the Dominican tyrant. Minerva's father is imprisoned, and she is taken into custody to be questioned about Lío's letters. Although father and daughter are released—with Don Enrique gravely ill as a result of his brutal imprisonment—Trujillo is not a forgiving man. He does allow Minerva to graduate from law school. But then he takes his revenge by denying her a license to practice. *Las Mariposas*, then, become more resolute in their opposition to the dictator. However, as their involvement in the underground increases, so does the danger that they'll face Trujillo's wrath. Eventually, Minerva and Mate are imprisoned, and the latter is tortured. The Mirabals have their properties confiscated. In the end, Trujillo rids himself of this nuisance after he wishes out loud for their elimination while attending a party. Their deaths constitute, in the despot's eyes, the price the Butterflies must pay for opposing his rule.

Such absolute power, however, can only be maintained through oppression. Dissent is not tolerated. It is suppressed in an immediate and forceful manner. This is how dictators maintain control. As a consequence, because of their fears, the Dominicans of *In the Time of the Butterflies* are subservient, eager to please *El Jefe*. The entire nation performs for Trujillo's benefit during the country's centennial celebration. Trujillo is honored during every public ceremony, whether or not he is present. Individuals constantly seek the dictator's approval. A relative of the Mirabals, Tío Chiche, made loaded dice out of the bones of Christopher Columbus—whose remains the Dominicans assert are buried in their country—in order to please the dictator. The mother, Doña Mercedes, writes a letter expressing the family's loyalty to Trujillo after her husband's death. Later, for the strongman to consider releasing Minerva and Mate from prison, the mother has to write another letter begging for leniency. Thus the reader sees how even the rebellious Mirabal family subjects itself to the whims of the despot.

Trujillo's regime, however, in spite of its inherent evil, is also seductive. His power, godlike, without apparent limits, makes him attractive, even sexy. The Dominican dictator conquers the heart of Lina Lovatón, an astonishingly beautiful high school student. Years later, during the Discovery Day Dance, although Minerva abhors the dictator, she describes him in highly complimentary terms. Her ambivalent feelings towards him surprise her: she finds him sexually appealing. Trujillo, however, uses sex as a weapon. Through it he brings the women he seduces, as well as those close to them, under his control. His libido runs amok. He employs Manuel Montoya, whose sole function is to procure attractive young women to satisfy the dictator's gargantuan sexual appetite. This is how Minerva first comes to his attention. Trujillo specifically requested her presence at the Discovery Day Dance. As Manuel Montoya escorts her to *El Jefe*'s table, the hushed crowd knowingly stares as the "sacrifice" parades before them (95). Although Minerva initially finds Trujillo attractive, the charm vanishes completely when, as their dance together concludes, he crudely thrusts his pelvis into her. Minerva decidedly rejects him, but this does not deter the dictator. After imprisoning her father, the despot's men suggest that Don Enrique can be released immediately if Minerva agrees to sleep with Trujillo. Minerva, in spite of her concern for her father, is aware that to submit to the dictator's desires would mean that he would control her forever. Thus, she refuses his offer, and the stage is set for their prolonged antagonism.

An interesting aspect of Alvarez's development of the dictatorship theme is that, although Trujillo's presence is felt throughout, he seldom appears as a character. In his stead, the reader encounters a myriad of agents who seek to please the tyrant. When Minerva is taken into custody after the Discovery Day Dance, Trujillo does not question her. Proxies for the despot, a general and a member of the secret police, conduct the interrogation. Later, Manuel Montoya enters the room to convey *El Jefe*'s offer to release Minerva's father in return for her favors. The coercion Minerva is subjected to constitutes a concerted effort in which all three of Trujillo's representatives play their part to persuade Minerva to please the dictator.

Peña is the most notable of Trujillo's proxies. A captain in Trujillo's police force, he embodies the worst elements of the dictatorship. He is subservient, crude, cruel, manipulating, and devious. He is capable of any act to please *El Jefe*. So unlikable is this character that Patria, the most tolerant of the sisters, refers to him as "evil" (204). When the sisters are released from prison, Peña monitors them closely. Later, as Trujillo expresses out loud that he needs someone to rid him of his "problem," Peña willingly becomes his instrument. Immediately, like a spider, he begins to spin his web (282). In the end, he accomplishes his objective, he eliminates *Las Mariposas*. Through proxies like Peña, a dictator can make his presence felt everywhere. Like tentacles of evil, Trujillo's henchmen bring terror into every home, village, town, neighborhood, and city.

In the novel, Rafael Trujillo exists somewhere between a theme and a character. As the latter, his appearances are brief and his characterization is kept deliberately low-key because the *idea* of Trujillo is more important than the man himself. The dictator appears infrequently in the novel, and his character, rather than being well-developed, is more of a caricature. Alvarez prefers to develop Trujillo as a theme. He remains much more powerful as such, casting fear not only among the people of the

Dominican Republic, but also in the pages of *In the Time of the Butterflies*. In fact, in the novel's closing scene, as Dedé envisions the ghosts of her family, the boots of his specter are overheard stomping about the house.

Another theme the novel explores is revolution. *In the Time of the Butterflies* is set during a time in Latin America's history when dictatorships were rampant, and young revolutionaries adamantly called for radical changes. Among these revolutionaries one stood out: Fidel Castro. The Cuban leader is another presence in Alvarez's novel. His deeds and words inhabit the thoughts of the Butterflies. They find inspiration in his example. Both Minerva and Dedé listen, in secret, to Fidel's speeches, transmitted over a clandestine Cuban radio station. In her novel, Alvarez includes Fidel's most recognized words: "Condemn me, it does not matter. History will absolve me" (125). This phrase, pronounced during Fidel's eloquent defense as he faced trial for leading a failed attack on the Moncada army barracks, helped make Castro a hero in the eyes of several generations of Latin Americans. The Butterflies admire his defiance of Fulgencio Batista, the dictator of neighboring Cuba. Later, the sisters rejoice when the Fidel's rebels overthrow Batista's regime. In fact, so deep is their admiration for Castro's accomplishment that Patria names her unborn son Raúl Ernesto—after Raúl Castro, Fidel's brother, and the Argentine revolutionary, Ernesto "Che" Guevara. In essence, the child represents the "new man" that the Cuban Revolution promulgates: an individual more interested in the betterment of society than in personal gain. Thus, Fidel and his revolution becomes the model for the Dominican underground. The idea of revolution, then, for those fighting against Trujillo's regime, is to replicate Castro's victory in Cuba. All this occurred when the Cuban Revolution was still in its infancy: before Castro declared the island a Marxist state, and before January 3, 1961, when diplomatic relationships between Cuba and the United States were severed.

Many times, however, the dreams and ideals of revolutionaries do not materialize. Every rebel deals with the risk of failure, of losing everything, including her or his life. Such is the case with *Las Mariposas*. In the end, though their deaths sparked the flame that would bring Trujillo's reign to a halt, what they set out to accomplish fell far short of its mark. Their plans fail miserably. The botched invasion, together with the collapse of the plot to assassinate Trujillo, place them in grave danger, and ultimately cost them their lives. After Minerva's release from prison, she becomes disillusioned with the idea of a revolution. She never fully recovers from the failure of her plans. Her husband, Manolo, doesn't recover either. He dies later hoping to change society. To add to the family's disillusionment, Dedé considers that his death was meaningless. In fact, in the epilogue, during an affluent gathering, amid a new generation of spoiled, apathetic Dominicans, she sadly wonders if the sacrifice her sisters made was not in vain.

In the Time of the Butterflies also explores the role of the Catholic Church in Dominican political affairs. Over the centuries in Latin America, the Catholic Church has been perceived as being in collusion with governments and the ruling classes. This perception is reinforced when the nuns, in not opposing the dictator's actions, allow his seduction of Lina Lovatón. Furthermore, as a reward for the school's collaboration, he constructs the Lina Lovatón Gymnasium. Later, in a superimposition that reflects the church's total alignment with Trujillo's regime, as Patria searches for the answers to her nation's ills, she stares at a portrait of Jesus. The image of Christ merges with a portrait of the dictator hanging beside it: they become one. Again, in a similar metaphor, Minerva describes a handheld fan that has a picture of Trujillo on one side, and one of the *Virgencita* on the reverse. In this superimposition the reader sees that the dictator has the backing of the Church: an endorsement that gives him a divine status.

In the novel, however, the Catholic Church undergoes a process of change. Alarmed with the desperate conditions that face the poor, some clergy in Latin America embraced what is known as liberation theology. The doctrine of liberation theology teaches that the Church must return to its origins, it must again become a Church of the Poor. The Church must cease to align itself with the rich and the powerful. It must commit wholeheartedly to the struggle for social justice. Under the doctrine of liberation theology, the Church has the obligation to raise the consciousness of the masses. The poor need to become aware of the abuses they suffer. They also need to unite in order to change, for themselves, oppressive economic and political systems. Although liberation theology rejects Marxism's atheist worldview, it draws heavily on Marxist analysis of the causes of poverty and oppression in underdeveloped nations. On the subject of armed struggle, while deploring all violence, liberation theologians taught that revolution, or counterviolence, is justified as a last resort against the greater violence of tyrants.

Indeed, the doctrine of liberation theology is present in Alvarez's work. After the nuns' acquiescence of Lina Lovatón's seduction, they redeem themselves, to a small degree, when they help hide Hilda, a young subversive, from Trujillo's police. However, liberation theology is introduced as a theme primarily through Patria's religiosity. In the first instance, during the Mirabal's pilgrimage to Higüey, the voice of the *Virgencita* tells Patria to look for her among the poor. Later, when Patria is worried about her son's growing enthusiasm for the underground, she finds no solace in the answers the Church has always given her. She turns to Padre de Jesús for help. The young priest confesses that he also lacks answers. Thus the reader witnesses the emergence of a new Church, a Church that is searching for new answers to old problems. Padre de Jesús, then, becomes the embodiment of liberation theology. During the mountain retreat the participants fully discuss the new doctrine. Furthermore, the women had already formed "Christian Cultural Groups" to work in the slums. These groups represent the activism the new doctrine preaches. From Dedé's viewpoint, the readers discover the extent of Padre de Jesús's full involvement in the underground as he helps by hiding weapons in his church. The new Church, the Church Militant, as Patria refers to it, is committed to change. It is fighting a war of faith against the "devil" incarnate, Rafael Leonidas Trujillo.

Both Minerva and Dedé are initially skeptical of the Church's resolve. They don't believe it will take a stand against Trujillo. The sisters are well aware that the Church and the oligarchy have collaborated with each other for centuries. When Patria informs Minerva of the changes taking place within the Church, of how the Church intends to oppose the dictatorship, the latter replies: "Ha! Your church will keep mum till kingdom come. . . . Not a peep to help the downtrodden" (158). Later, though, Minerva becomes a firm believer in the Church's commitment to change. Dedé, on the other hand, is at first troubled by the "noise" coming from the Church's new militancy. But faced with the problems in her marriage, and later feeling in "harmony" with what the new Church is preaching, she decides to turn to it for answers (182). The split between Church and state is best illustrated when the mother separates the portraits of Jesus and Trujillo that have been hanging side by side in her home for years.

Of course, the commitment the new Church has made to change Dominican society places it on a collision course with Rafael Trujillo. It is not long before the dictator counterattacks. He begins by arresting Padre de Jesús. But the Church responds by replacing him with the equally radical Padre Gabriel. During the first mass that Padre Gabriel celebrates in the parish, he reads a sermon, authored by the nation's bishops, which condemns Trujillo's government. In response, the SIM, the despot's secret police, begins a physical attack upon the Church. This tactic proves disastrous. Dominicans begin to side openly with the Church. It gains new converts, such as Noris, Patria's daughter, who steps forward to help the Church recover from an attack. In this manner, Alvarez introduces the role of Catholicism in revolutions, a theme that has been a significant topic of discussion in contemporary Latin American studies.

In the Time of the Butterflies, like all of Alvarez's novels, explores the theme of machismo. The concept of machismo connotes a man's strength, bravery, power, and importance. These qualities represent the embodiment of the ideal male within a patriarchal society. Thus, in a patriarchy, machismo is institutionalized. Man rules over woman. A man has the power and the authority to make decisions for the women under his protectorate. Thus, men feel entitled to control the behavior of women. Because of this control, gender roles are strictly prescribed in such a society, with many professions, privileges, and freedoms denied to women.

Many of the male characters in the novel are domineering, including Trujillo himself. These men attempt to control the lives of their daughters and mates. Undoubtedly, the character that best exemplifies macho behavior is Dedé's husband, Jaimito. He is excessively controlling. In fact, the narrative explains that his machismo is largely to blame for their crumbling marriage (175). When Dedé asks Jaimito's permission for the underground to meet on their farm, he angrily refuses; he also demands that Dedé keep a distance from her siblings. His machismo is evident when the narrative describes his refusal with the following metaphor: "The Mirabal sisters liked to run their men, that was the problem. In his house, he was the one to wear the pants" (176–77). Jaimito becomes more domineering with the passage of time. He is extremely possessive of his four sons, naming each one after himself. In addition, when Dedé threatens to leave him, Jaimito responds with a threat of his own: to take the boys away from her. The fear of losing her sons forces Dedé to remain subservient to his wishes. But Jaimito not only exerts his authority over Dedé, he also exerts it over his mother and sisters. The only male in his family, he rules over the women with an iron fist. Although Dedé appears to submit to Jaimito, the narrative reveals that, in fact, she has been leading his mother and sisters in a quiet rebellion against his tyranny. Even Minerva, whose independence stands in direct opposition to Dedé's situation, recognizes the seriousness of her sister's dilemma when she absolves her from participating in the underground.

Other male characters also exhibit macho traits. Don Enrique Mirabal, the patriarch, at times attempts to dominate his family. He is opposed initially to his daughters' schooling. He firmly believes that women don't need an education and that, furthermore, they should remain close to the homestead. Alvarez employs the simile of the caged rabbits to convey to her readers Minerva's lifelong feeling of captivity as a result of her father's beliefs. After Minerva had graduated from high school, under the guise of protecting her, Don Enrique hides Lío's letters. This infuriates Minerva who, of course, feels that she doesn't need anyone's protection. In addition, she resents the invasion of her privacy. However, Don Enrique, as the family patriarch, sees it as his right as well as his obligation to intervene in such a manner in his daughters' lives.

In a macho society, double standards exist with regard to sexuality. There is considerable tolerance for, even approval of, a man's sexual escapades. Women, however, are forbidden from experiencing the same. Thus, married men can have affairs without fear of the consequences. Don Enrique, the Mirabal patriarch, has a mistress and a second family. He goes on mysterious trips supposedly to talk to the *campesinos* that live and work on his farm. Although his extramarital activities estrange him from his wife, she has little option but to tolerate his infidelity and maintain the appearance that the Mirabals are a happy family. The same occurs with Manolo and Minerva. He has an extramarital affair that deeply hurts her. However, Minerva, in spite of being the most independent and strong of all the characters, gladly welcomes Manolo back after the affair ends.

In a patriarchal society, men are expected to experiment with their sexuality at a young age. When Patria discovers that her seventeen-year-old son, Nelson, is having sex with a young widow, she asks Pedro to speak to him. Pedro, however, instead of being alarmed by his son's activity, reacts with pride at the boy's early entry into the sexual world. In fact, later, Patria also expresses her approval of her son's sexual education. She is grateful toward the young woman who delivered Nelson "gently into manhood" (152).

A macho society will often pit women against each other. Mate, for one, abhors the idea of her father's mistress and of her half-sisters. She becomes furious when they show up at his funeral. Rather than observing the mistress and her daughters as victims of Don Enrique's machismo, Mate sees them as rivals, as her enemies. Ironically, the half-sisters later play a vital role when Minerva and Mate are in prison. Through Don Enrique's illegitimate children the Mirabals are able to send and receive messages from the prisoners. In this way, the half-sisters repay Minerva's generosity and her acceptance of them as family.

The reader also learns that both Minerva and Dedé helped pay for the education of the oldest half-sister. In fact, Patria, although at the onset angry at the woman who did not respect the "holy banns of matrimony," is hurt to discover that she was left out of the arrangement, for she would have liked to have helped (209). Thus, we see how the Mirabal sisters are able to overcome the cultural prejudices regarding machismo to help their father's other family.

Machismo, the narrative reminds us, is not entirely negative. In spite of Jaimito's fervent machismo, he also possesses certain traits that, to a small degree, redeem him. After learning that Dedé had gone to see Padre de Jesús to talk about their marital problems, Jaimito is eager to understand her concerns as well as to learn how to behave differently. Unfortunately, just as the spouses agree to seek a resolution to their differences, the world of the Mirabal family collapses. The ensuing calamities, however, bring out the best in Jaimito. When the members of the underground are arrested, he fulfills a positive role, taking care of the "womenfolk" and looking after the families of the men who are now in prison (196). Patria offers us the most sympathetic view of Jaimito. Under all his macho bravado, she sees a big heart (211–12). Thus, we see a positive side of machismo—a side that can be strong, caring, and responsible.

A LIMINAL READING OF *IN THE TIME OF THE BUTTERFLIES*

Liminality, a term first used by the anthropologist Arnold van Gennep in 1908, refers to one of the stages of "rites of passages." A rite of passage is a ritual associated with a crisis or a change of status in the life of an individual or a group. Marriage, illness, revolution, and death are but a few among numerous rites of passages. The first stage in a rite of passage is that of "separation," which comprises the detachment of the individual or the group from the social mainstream. In the second liminal stage, liminal entities are neither here nor there. Victor Turner (1974), van Gennep's successor in the study of liminality, states that liminal entities "are betwixt and between the positions assigned and arrayed by law, customs, conventions, and ceremonial" (The Ritual Process 95). The third and final stage in a rite of passage is that of reaggregation, whereby the subject (or subjects) reenters the social structure. For van Gennep, liminality constituted a phase, an ephemeral moment destined to be superseded. Turner added a synchronic, or time dimension, to the notion. He argued that liminality must be looked upon not only as a transition but as a state in itself, as the liminal "moment" can conceivably turn into a permanent condition. Thus, where van Gennep thinks of liminality as only a threshold, Turner sees it also as a place of habitation. Both anthropologists agree, however, that liminality constitutes an indeterminate, transitory space where the subject is being worked on as it awaits its reaggregation into society.

The concept of liminality can be easily applied to literary studies. It is employed to identify and explain the liminal stages in the development of a character, a plot, or situation. Liminality abounds in literature. Characters are often dislocated, confused with respect to their identities, and undergo ordeals and educational experiences that accurately reflect anthropological liminal phases. The same occurs with a character's reaggregation, or acceptance, into a society.

Sacrifices, rebellions, imprisonments, madness, fear, violence, changes in identities, and existences as symbols are indicative of the liminal experience as well. Furthermore, liminality is associated with a profound change in outlook of the characters, and perhaps of the society they represent. It comes, then, as no surprise that critics have used the concept of liminality in studying a wide range of world literatures and literary periods.

In the Time of the Butterflies lends itself perfectly to a liminal reading. The Mirabal sisters, the government of the Dominican Republic, the Church, as well as the narrative itself are, for the greater part of the novel, suspended in a liminal state—betwixt and between what they were and what they are to become. As discussed earlier in the section on characterization, the reader witnesses the sisters' various transformations: their loss of innocence, their political awakening, and their commitment to become revolutionaries.

From the moment Minerva slaps the dictator, after she is presented as a sacrifice in a highly ritualistic setting, the Butterflies will exist in a liminal state. They enter the world of ideals, which clash with the despot's, and their vision of a just society now depends on their activism. Thus, they have become, in essence, revolutionaries, and as such they live on the margins of the mainstream. However, this constitutes a transitory state. Soon after the underground's plot to eliminate Trujillo fails, Minerva and Mate are imprisoned, separated from society, and forcefully removed from the revolution. After their release, the Butterflies, now including Patria, exist in a total state of detachment. They are not allowed trips, visitors, or contact with other known dissidents.

While the Mirabal sisters are housebound, they enter yet another liminal state. They are neither prisoners nor free; they neither cooperate with Trujillo, nor can they now rebel against him. In other words, to quote Victor Turner they "are betwixt and between the positions assigned and arrayed by law, customs, conventions, and ceremon[y]." However, without their knowledge or consent, their reaggregation into Dominican society has already taken place. During their brief outings they discover that they are treated with reverence. Minerva, in particular, is uncomfortable with the veneration. But there is nothing she can do about it. She and her sisters are the subjects being acted upon at society's will. The Mirabals have, to use an obvious metaphor, exited their cocoons and reentered society as *Las Mariposas*. Their once secret code name now represents an integral part of their identities. In barely audible whispers, wherever they go, people salute them with the phrase, ¡*Vivan las Mariposas!*. Their resistance to Trujillo, their incarceration, and more importantly, their survival, has made them icons of hope. Their status as heroines of the resistance is one they never anticipated, as well as one that they accept with great reluctance, for they intuitively know that as butterflies, although beautiful, they are also fragile, ethereal.

Their new standing within Dominican society, however, also gives rise to their next metamorphosis, setting up the stage for their final rite of passage. The last thing Dominican dictator Rafael Trujillo intended was for the three dissidents to become symbols of resistance. The Butterflies, although themselves exhausted and somewhat disillusioned, are inspiring others to oppose the strongman's regime. Unwittingly, the dictator's tactics made them far more dangerous than they were prior to their imprisonment. Trujillo can do little but wish out loud that this "problem" be eliminated—and his wish is granted. However, with their deaths, Trujillo creates an infinitely more dangerous symbol. While frail and vulnerable in life, in death the Butterflies have become invincible. Trujillo, with all his apparatus of terror and death, can no longer prevent their ideals from reaching fruition. The sisters have been reaggregated into Dominican society as myths, legends, martyrs, and saints. The Dominican people place their faith in the sisters' spirits. They believe the Butterflies perform miracles. The price for the murder of the Mirabal sisters is very high indeed: the dictator's own life. His cronies in the military realize this, and they willingly deliver on the payment.

On the other hand, Dedé, the sister who survived, exists in a state apart from her siblings. She is utterly alone in her liminality. She refuses to become involved in the underground. A cautious individual, she is not willing to take the same risks as her sisters. She lives on the margins of their revolution—listening and watching, but doing nothing. How-

ever, once Minerva and Mate are imprisoned, Dedé realizes that her fate
has been bound up to theirs all along. By remaining detached from the
underground Dedé saves herself from facing Trujillo's wrath, but she
still experiences every bit of her sisters' anguish. As it turns out, Dedé
has been living her entire life in a liminal state: she has been betwixt and
between any meaningful position. Once her sisters are imprisoned, however, she becomes their anchor. Dedé reenters society as the leader of
the Mirabals, offering strength and stability when the family most
needs it.

With the deaths of the Butterflies, however, Dedé enters another liminal state. The pain of her beloved sisters' death paralyzes her. Shortly
after the tragedy, the only role she can fulfill is as the sister who survived—a role she assumes by virtue of her abstention from politics.
Nevertheless, this assignment constitutes a permanent state. Dedé's des-
ignation as the surviving sister makes her uncomfortable, but she has no
alternative. Like her sisters before her, she is the subject being worked
on as she awaits her reaggregation into society. Inherently, the label of
the sister who survived has little worth. Nevertheless, she must learn to
live with it in the hope that someday it will become useful. For a time
Dedé becomes the depository of peoples' stories about *Las Mariposas*,
particularly those who witnessed their last hours of life. Dedé absorbs
these tales, not knowing where they will lead. But she senses that the
act of listening forms part of a rite of passage. In time, she too experiences a metamorphosis. She awakens to the need of telling the story of
her sisters—for her own sake as well as for the sake of the Dominican
people. In this manner Dedé exits the liminal state and reenters society
as the oracle and guardian of the Butterflies' legacy. Her mission is not
to let their deaths, nor the deaths of other Dominicans who have opposed
tyranny, be in vain.

Other entities in the novel can also be examined under the scope of
liminality. For instance, the *gringa dominicana*, throughout the narrative,
exists in a liminal state. She is neither a *gringa* (American) nor a *dominicana* (Dominican) but rather someone who dwells, uneasily, between
cultures. Her Dominican side fully appreciates the profound significance
of the story of the Butterflies. However, she cannot transcribe it in the
language in which it was lived. Therefore, she intends to translate the
story so that an American audience can read about this tragedy. Thus,
as the interview woman gathers information from Dedé, the details
themselves exist in a liminal state: they exist in translation. The *gringa
dominicana*'s task is to try to filter the data into another language for

consumption by people of an alien culture. Her translation, in fact, goes very well. The more the interview woman succeeds in her goal of making the story accessible to English speakers, the more she fades into the background, until she virtually disappears. She seamlessly weaves two cultures together. In this manner, as the interview woman accomplishes her retrieval of the story, she is reaggregated into a new identity: the *gringa dominicana* becomes the bridge through space, time, languages, and cultures that allows Americans to experience the legacy of *Las Mariposas*.

The Catholic Church also undergoes a transformation. At the onset of the novel, the reader encounters a Church functioning in its traditional role as it collaborates with the country's ruling class. However, members of the clergy soon realize that the Church can no longer condone the injustices of Trujillo's regime. Thus, to better understand the role the Church must play in correcting the wrongs of Dominican society, they separate themselves from the mainstream. Young priests, like Padre de Jesús, admit that they lack immediate solutions to old problems. But while the Church is in this liminal state, it is also searching. Appropriately, during a retreat, another separation from society, the Church finds its answer in liberation theology. Patria and Padre de Jesús descend from the mountain with a clear view of what needs to be done. The Mother Church has now become the Church Militant, and it is ready to reenter society in a decisive, forceful manner.

In the novel, the reader finds that the Dominican Republic is also in a liminal state. Initially the nation is an absolute dictatorship. Trujillo rules with unquestioned authority. Every citizen cooperates with the regime, either willingly, or out of the need to survive. Not far into the novel, however, opposition to Trujillo begins to grow, and the dictator reacts forcefully against the dissidents. His repressive tactics draws international attention, and the Organization of American States (OAS), through an embargo, separates the Dominican Republic from this league of nations. In this manner the country begins its liminal existence. A dictatorship is about to exit, but a democracy still remains a dream. Even after Trujillo's death, and the Dominican Republic's reaggregation into the society of nations, it continues to exist in a liminal state. In the epilogue of *In the Time of the Butterflies*, the reader observes how the country has made strides toward the establishment of an honest, productive, and democratic society. However, the reader also can determine, in light of Dedé's disenchantment, that the Dominican Republic still has a way to go to achieve the objective for which *Las Mariposas* gave their lives.

One of the central features in Turner's studies on liminality is the formation of *communitas* among liminal entities. In Turner's construct, *communitas* constitutes the relationships between people who are undergoing transition. The bonds of *communitas* are anti-structural in the sense that relationships are undifferentiated and egalitarian. According to Turner, the formation of a *communitas* among liminal entities is spontaneous, immediate, and concrete. *Communitas* are not shaped by norms, or institutionalized, or abstract (Dramas 174). Such *communitas* do exist in the novel. For instance, as revolutionaries, the Butterflies exist in a liminal state. In trying to change society, what they intend to do is to make the mainstream embrace their ideals. Thus, as liminal entities on the margins of traditional thinking, the underground becomes their *communitas*. Here, revolutionaries bond with others who, like them, are separated from society as they await their reentry into a transformed mainstream. The same occurs with Minerva and Mate while they are in prison; they become part of a *communitas* of cellmates. The relationships between inmates, regardless of what they have been incarcerated for, are undifferentiated and egalitarian. The bonds formed in prison became of great significance to the sisters. Both Minerva and Mate shed tears of sadness when they leave behind their prison *communitas* in route to experience their next transformation.

Under two separate sets of circumstances, the Butterflies undertake pilgrimages. Studies, both anthropological and literary, demonstrate that pilgrimage sites are located on the margins or borders of mainstream population centers. In addition, Turner states that the actor–pilgrims who are involved in such journeys participate in symbolic activities that they believe will change their inner conditions from sin to grace, from strife to peace, from sickness to health. Pilgrims hope for miracles or transformations, either of the body or the soul (Dramas 197–98). Indeed, the sisters first make a pilgrimage to a site where the *Virgencita* is said to have appeared. Although each Mirabal woman has a petition to make, Patria, in particular, is hoping for a profound change in her inner self to take place. She wants to move from sin to grace, from strife to peace. This pilgrimage site is located far from the mainstream, in a small community of poor, desperate people. It is here that Patria recovers her faith. The voice of the *Virgencita* tells the eldest of the Mirabal sisters to look for her among the *communitas* of the dispossessed.

The set of second pilgrimages the Butterflies undertake are the visits to their jailed husbands. Their stated goal here is to save their men. However, as the reader knows, these pilgrimages lead to their deaths. Far from the mainstream, as they cross over the mountain pass, *Las Mar-*

iposas are abducted and slain. Ironically, their martyrdom initiates another steady stream of pilgrims who, like the narrative informs us, travel from all over the world to visit Dedé in order to learn more about the Butterflies. Alvarez, in writing *In the Time of the Butterflies*, in essence also takes the reader on this pilgrimage. And as pilgrims, the readers hope to witness the miracle of the Mirabal's sacrifice to make this a better world.

As the title of the novel indicates, the narrative is frozen in time. The story contained within the pages of *In the Time of the Butterflies* represents a turbulent epoch in the history of the Dominican Republic. It is a time that remains painfully etched in the minds of many Dominicans. Although Dedé tries to focus on the happy times in the lives of the Mirabal family, her memories invariably take her back to the time of the Butterflies, the saddest time of her life, a time that marked her forever. In her second novel, Julia Alvarez seeks to take her readers into the heart and spirit of these times. In addition, in the Postscript, Alvarez states her intention to rescue the Mirabal sisters from their legendary status. She hopes to restore their humanity. The Dominican-American also hopes to make their heroism accessible to everyone. In essence, she wants to remove *Las Mariposas* from their liminal state, from the lofty height of a virtually unreachable pedestal upon which their sacrifice has placed them.

At the onset of *In the Time of the Butterflies*, Fela serves as medium for the sisters. Soon, however, the Mirabal sisters stop visiting the faithful Haitian maid. Fela informs Minou, Minerva's daughter, that perhaps the Butterflies have finally been put to rest. Perhaps Alvarez's vibrant and compelling novel will, in fact, help *Las Mariposas*—Dedé included—exit their liminal state and at last find peace.

5

¡Yo!
(1997)

In *How the García Girls Lost Their Accents*, the narrator does not spare the feelings of her subjects. Yo tells the family story in its entirety, blemishes and all. In Alvarez's inaugural work, the pain of expatriation resides alongside the joys of the characters' discovery of their new selves as they adapt, seldom without trauma, to a new country, a new culture, and a new language. The readers witness how cultural displacement, rather than uniting a family, can serve as a divisive force.

Alvarez's third novel, *¡Yo!* (once again published by Algonquin Books of Chapel Hill), perhaps represents her greatest feat as a novelist. This work further examines the life of Yolanda María Teresa García de la Torre, the narrator of *How the García Girls Lost Their Accents*. The problem for Yo, however, is that now the tables have been turned on her. The characters whose secrets she betrayed in the first novel want their revenge. And others are poised to join in. Instead of having the freedom to continue as the storyteller, she is now the subject of sixteen different characters who seek to paint the portrait, unflattering at times, of the artist.

Like Miguel de Cervantes's *Don Quixote de la Mancha*, *¡Yo!* begins with the characters' acute awareness of themselves as literary personages. They know that they have been written about, and they are not happy about it. Angered at their lives being appropriated for fictional fodder, the members of the García family are enraged and horrified at Yo's newfound celebrity status. Yo is constantly on book tours, she appears on television talk shows to continue exposing the family dirt, her "novel" is studied in college classrooms and, worst of all, family members can no longer speak to her without first contacting her literary agent. But this is only the beginning.

Progressing through fifteen more exposés on Yo, the reader hears from a cousin, a former teacher, a former student whose story she plagiarized in order to receive tenure, and Dominican *campesinos* whose lives she impacted during writing retreats in her country of birth. Even heard from is a mentally disturbed stalker who has pursued Yo for years and whose obsession with the author has increased thanks to her fame. The stories charm, enchant, and at times bewilder the reader. Yo, as portrayed by these wonderfully constructed and varied narrative voices, is a complex individual. She is vulnerable and very sensitive to any sort of criticism. Yet she can also be remarkably strong when confronted with injustices, poverty, death, and abusive or failed relationships.

What emerges from the narrative is a skewed portrait of the artist, one that is full of contradictions that in some instances seem irreconcilable. Still, the stories are told with Alvarez's key signatures: humor, passion, and compassion. At the end, readers sense that they have experienced an astounding narrative juggling act. Like Miguel de Cervantes, Julia Alvarez knows that humor can probe deeply into tales of startling truths and wisdom. And also like Cervantes, she performs a literary miracle.

PLOT DEVELOPMENT AND STRUCTURE

In the traditional sense, like in Julia Alvarez's first novel, the reader will not find a plot in ¡*Yo!*. The organization of incident and character in ¡*Yo!*, as in *How the García Girls Lost Their Accents*, is episodic. However, while the structure of Alvarez's debut novel challenges the reader, ¡*Yo!* reads in a straightforward manner. Each chapter stands alone as a well-developed story with a recognizable plot. Yet, in spite of being episodic, the novel has remarkable unity. The reader never feels lost or frustrated. Rather than developing a traditional plot, Alvarez opts to take her readers on a chronological journey through the life of Yolanda García, as seen through the eyes of others.

The events related in ¡*Yo!*, however, begin in the present of the narrative. The Garcías are angry at Yo because she has revealed family secrets in her best-selling novel. She has succeeded as a writer, but at the cost of alienating those closest to her. The narrative then travels back in time to the "Bear" incident, which serves as a bridge between the Garcías' previous life in the Dominican Republic and their new beginning in the United States. Subsequent chapters explore Yo's high school experience, her college years, her indecision about becoming a writer, her failed marriages, her ensuing difficulty in establishing relationships with men, her decision to become a writer, her commitment to learning the craft, her writing retreats in the Dominican Republic, her career as a college teacher, her struggles to earn tenure, her third marriage, her feelings about motherhood, her fears of being a stepmother, and her success as a writer.

Structurally, the novel consists of sixteen chapters, with the first chapter serving as a prologue. The remainder of the work is divided symmetrically into three parts consisting of five chapters each. The prologue begins at the present of the narrative. It describes the effect that the success of Yo's first novel is having upon the García clan. Part I of *¡Yo!* begins with the family's first few weeks in the United States. From there it moves in chronological order through Yo's life as seen by others. The concluding chapter of Part III, "The Father," brings the structure of the novel full circle. Like the Prologue, the final chapter also takes place in the present of the narrative. In this chapter, the father offers a blessing so that Yo, and hopefully her family, can be at peace with her need to tell stories. As the reader can observe, unlike Alvarez's first novel, the structure of *¡Yo!* is neat and tidy. The events, themes, and recurring characters provide the narrative with unity. Of course, Yo's presence in every chapter provides the novel its cohesiveness. In the end, although *¡Yo!* can be considered an experimental novel, Alvarez's development of the plot as well as the structure of her work fully engage the reader.

POINT OF VIEW

¡Yo! constitutes an ingenious reversal of how Alvarez employed the point of view in *How the García Girls Lost Their Accents*. In the Dominican-American's first novel, readers learn, at the conclusion, that they have been viewing the stories from Yolanda's perspective all along. She, a bona fide storyteller, takes considerable license in assuming the voices of the other family members. This time around, however, the story has been wrested away from Yo. She has lost control of the storytelling process. In fact, Yolanda García has been rendered powerless. She is now

the subject of sixteen different characters that offer their perspectives of the effect that she—and her need to tell stories—has had on their lives.

The points of view in ¡Yo! shift between the first-person and the third-person limited. Of the novel's sixteen chapters, eight employ the first-person viewpoint, seven the third-person limited, and one mixes both. Alvarez's use of the shifting viewpoint keeps the narrative engaging. An interesting example that illustrates the Dominican-American's mastery of the use of viewpoint is the chapter titled "The Wedding Guests." The narrative begins with the third-person limited viewpoint of Luke, the minister who is about to officiate the wedding ceremony. Presiding over the event, he is, in comparison to the wedding guests, detached from the feelings of others as well as from his own. His primary concern is over what he will say during the ceremony. From the emotional distance of the third-person point of view, Luke offers the reader several observations about the guests. He reflects on the anger in Yo's soon-to-be step-daughter, the goodness of the groom's parents, and the cultural differences between the subdued members of his congregation and Yo's raucous Dominican relatives. The Lutheran minister's distant, somewhat panoramic viewpoint also lets the reader know that several characters from previous stories are present. As overseer of the event, Luke also wonders how such disparate personalities are ever going to blend together.

The narrative then shifts to the first-person perspective. The viewpoint will jump through a succession of characters who share their most intimate thoughts: Corey, Dexter, Doug, Sara, Tía Flor, Lucinda, and Tammy. Each character expresses his or her take on Yo, kind or not. They also share with us their own hopes, fears, prejudices, jealousies, frustrations, and disappointments. The narrative then completes a full circle, returning to the third-person limited viewpoint of the minister as everyone begins to congregate for the ceremony. This chapter represents a tour de force in Alvarez's use of the shifting viewpoint. "The Wedding Guests" constitutes a veritable workshop on how to position a narrator in relation to an event. More importantly, in spite of Alvarez's experimentation, the reader never feels lost with her use of the wandering viewpoint. Quite the contrary, one finds the experience highly engaging.

There is, in ¡Yo!, another notable chapter with respect to Alvarez's employment of the point of view. In "The Stalker," the Dominican-American writer takes her readers on a disturbing as well as realistic voyage into the deranged, obsessive mind of an individual intent on capturing Yo's attention. This chapter lacks Alvarez's usual poetic narrative. The character's thoughts are presented in prose that is intense, raw, and on edge. The stalker's thoughts, as well as the events narrated within the chapter, flash before the reader, all occurring in rapid succession. In addition, the stalker's viewpoint is focused inward. It is an absolutely egotistical viewpoint. He fails to grasp completely the effect his behavior and words have on others. The reader notes that the only word ever capitalized in the narrative is the first-person pronoun, "I." Furthermore, the lack of punctuation, the lack of a coherent, logical, and fluid narrative heightens the sense of danger that Yo faces. Alvarez's technique makes the experience a frightening one. The reader huddles around Yo, and hopes that she survives intact into the final chapter.

Through the use of a wide array of viewpoints, Alvarez creates a complex look into Yo's character. True to life, sixteen different perspectives offer the reader sixteen different takes on Yo, and at times these perspectives clash with one another. Thus, in the end, thanks to the Dominican-American's adept use of the point of view, what emerges is an engaging, yet profound look into the life and character of Yolanda García—warts and all.

CHARACTER DEVELOPMENT

Yolanda García, as indicated in the title, is the central character of Julia Alvarez's second novel. Yo's life and her need to be the storyteller affect the other characters. In spite of many of the characters being dynamic— that is, fully developed—Yo emerges as the most complex one of all. What the supporting characters provide, with their individual biases, is a multidimensional look into Yo. Their impressions, all sixteen of them, of the novel's central character, form a kaleidoscope, a shifting display of perspectives, through which the reader can gaze at Yo. Their takes on Yo are varied, each told from a different perspective. Thus her portrait is always moving, always mutable. The readers, then, become responsible for gleaning through all the viewpoints to try to arrive at their own conclusions on Yolanda García.

¡Yo! finds Julia Alvarez at her peak with regard to character development. She ingeniously develops Yo by way of the traits with which the other characters endow her, and the manner in which they describe how Yo puts these traits to work. Thus, Alvarez, through the novel's supporting characters, ably portrays all four sides of Yolanda García: her general, physical, personal, and emotional nature.

When the reader first encounters Yo, in this follow-up to *How the García Girls Lost Their Accents*, she has become a successful author. Her first novel is a best-seller. She travels around the country on book tours. Furthermore, she is now part of the radio and television talk-show circuits. However, her fame comes with a price: the Garcías are angry at Yo for having raided their family history. Their "plagiarized" lives are now part of the public domain (7). The Garcías resent her spiel about how art and life mirror each other. They consider it a mere excuse for her theft of their stories. Moreover, they complain about how she talks about the family as if it were made-up characters. But regardless of their bitterness toward Yo's literary pillage, they still definitely love her. When the García's gather to celebrate the birth of Sandi's baby, they feel hollow, empty because of Yolanda's absence. There is, though, one family member that approves of her endeavors. In the novel's final chapter, Yo's father expresses his unabashed pride at his daughter's success. He calls her books his "grandbabies" (294). Thus, the reader knows that the García family will reconcile with Yo in spite of her literary raids into their private lives.

Yo, since childhood, has been the family storyteller. From her mother's perspective, she has always been the habitual liar in the family. Yo, however, is obsessed with telling stories. She even builds upon the stories of others. For instance, Sara, the maid's daughter, confesses how she had become a mysterious rich girl in the eyes of her schoolmates. Yo is delighted by this unintentional deception. To aggravate matters, while Yo observes Sara in school as part of a college project on acculturation, the writer embellishes on the lie, making the maid's daughter even more intriguing in the eyes of her teachers. Yo's enhancement of Sara's story make it emotionally impossible for the young girl to sustain the deception. Because of Yo's need to invent stories, Sara is forced to ask for Laura's permission, as well as her financial assistance, in order to attend a private school.

Yo cannot resist manipulating the stories of others. During her wedding, Yo is intent on weaving together the tales of a very disparate group of people. In her eyes, this has the potential to become one of her best narrative fabrications. According to the minister's perspective, the guests resemble what constitutes the essence of the novel: "a kaleidoscope of colors," "a quilting of lives, a collection of points of view" (216). Yo hovers over this gathering as master storyteller, hoping that their individual stories will come together to form a beautiful work of fiction that she can later claim as her own.

Yo's desire to control the storytelling process makes it imperative for her to have the last word—always. This aspect of her characterization places her in constant conflict with others, particularly her family. On several occasions, Laura, Yo's mother, threatens to use Tabasco sauce on her daughter's smart mouth. Sandi, her sister, also knows well of Yo's penchant for having the last word. This is why after they had not spoken to each other for several months on account of Yo's writings, Sandi finally breaks the silence by telling her side of the story to Yo's answering machine. In this manner she is guaranteed to have her version respected, free from her sister's tampering.

A storyteller requires certain personal traits in order to be successful in her craft. And Yo certainly is endowed with these. She is intelligent, observant, insightful, and curious about the essence of everything. As a child, Yo was the first sister to figure out that the bear coming out of the closet was her mother in disguise. This discovery didn't surprise Laura who was well acquainted with her daughter's intelligence. In fact, Laura claims that shortly after the family's arrival to the United States, Yo was the only person who could see right through her to spot the terrified woman inside. Yo's father states that of all of the sisters, she is most like him because she tries to answer the impossible questions. This, the reader learns, is how she gains access into the secret heart of the other characters.

Yo reveals an early awareness that her destiny is to become a writer. In spite of this, she is unsure in embracing it. In fact, Alvarez's character can be extremely insecure overall. Her college mentor, Professor Garfield, spends decades dealing with Yo's indecisiveness. Although he is somewhat responsible for her insecurity—by repeatedly counseling her to become a scholar rather than an author—it is he who eventually pushes her out of the nest. Jordan Garfield orders Yolanda to write, write, write. She, once again, expresses her insecurities, stating that she doesn't know if she can do it. To her self-doubts, the professor succinctly replies: "You don't have a choice" (96). Thus, it is Professor Garfield's resolve, and not his former student's, which propels Yo to embrace her destiny.

Yolanda is extremely sensitive, emotional, and vulnerable. In the novel's first chapter, a weepy Yo calls her sister Fifi to cry about how the family has ostracized her. Other characters also react to Yo's emotional vulnerability. When she is on the verge of earning tenure, her plagiarized student, initially angered by the theft of his story, remembers her helplessness when she was a young, untenured professor. He then surprises himself when instead of denouncing Yo's dishonesty, he endorses her quest for permanence.

On the other hand, Yolanda García can also be seen as a strong, determined individual. Marie, the landlady, witnesses this when Yo announces that she is moving out of the apartment because of the marital strife between the landlords. Marie argues that Yo cannot break the lease. The strength and determination in Yo's stare shocks the landlady: "I have never seen a woman look like that before, though I have seen plenty of men with them surefire eyes" (162). Further proof of Yo's resolve is that she earned tenure, in spite of the college's good ol' boys network and her being the only Latina woman in an academic community that is culturally homogeneous.

As in *How the García Girls Lost Their Accents*, Yo continues to suffer from cultural displacement, but to a much lesser degree. The suitor, Dexter, observes how Yo is caught between two worlds. At the time, although she has been living in the United States for twenty-five years, she still calls the Dominican Republic home. However, as Dexter points out, Yo loves, has friends, pays taxes, and will probably die in the United States. Later, Doug, her third husband, tells of Yo's difficulty readjusting to the United States whenever she returns from the island. In spite of Yo's successful assimilation into the culture of the United States, she is still dealing with the problem of trying to find her place.

The Dominican characters, however, give us an entirely different portrait of the artist. The prism though which these characters examine Yo is diametrically opposed to their U.S. counterparts. The people that Yo comes in contact with during her writing retreats are afflicted by poverty and illiteracy. Moreover, she puzzles them. Yo is a hybrid, existing between cultures and languages. Unlike the members of the Dominican upper class, Yo is easygoing. She treats poor people with respect. In fact, the Dominican characters agree that Yo is "not from the usual run of rich ladies" (102). The *campesinos*, or farm workers, enjoy working for her. Yo is a true egalitarian. She treats rural Dominicans as equals. They also see her as generous. She helps them write letters or gives them employment. So great is their trust in Yo that the villagers use her as their advocate when the church group from the United States arrives to build a house. These Dominicans do not accept the gift until Yo gives her approval.

In the eyes of Dominicans, however, Yo's foreignness makes her appear eccentric. Poor Dominicans are not accustomed to someone of a higher socio-economic status being so talkative, so interested in what they have to say. They would never expect to be offered Cokes served in fine glasses full of ice. Her profession, a writer, is meaningless to people who can't read. Furthermore, her American ways bewilder them. In fact, it becomes a great cause of concern, as well as a source of humor, when the village men learn that Yo's husband has undergone a vasectomy. They are ignorant regarding the nature of this procedure. Dominicans are already convinced that *Americanos* are "not good at satisfying their women" (246). So, to confuse matters even more, they believe that Yo will never find marital satisfaction because her husband had himself castrated. This episode highlights the cultural as well as educational gaps that exist between the Dominican characters and their American counterparts. In addition, it shines a different light on Yo, a character the reader gets to observe through seemingly infinite lenses.

LITERARY DEVICE: ANAGNORISIS

Anagnorisis is the Greek term for "recognition" or "discovery" that Aristotle uses in his work, *Poetics*. It denotes the turning point in a drama during which a character awakens to the true state of affairs, having been previously in error or ignorance. The plots of many novels involve crucial anagnorises, also referred to as "the moment of truth." A novel can have many anagnorises, including a final one that supersedes all the others. Each anagnorisis reveals something to a character; and it reveals something about her or him as well.

In *¡Yo!*, Julia Alvarez spends considerable effort providing anagnorises for the supporting characters. Virtually every one of them has a moment of recognition, when ignorance or error gives way to knowledge. For instance, Fifi, the youngest sister, at first angry at Yo's revelations about the family's history, becomes calm after seeing her husband Otto's nonchalance about the whole incident. The husband's response awakens her to her family's disproportionate reaction. Later, when the Garcías gather to celebrate the birth of Sandi's child, they experience a collective anagnorisis when they feel the great void caused by Yo's absence. They awaken to their need to include her once again as part of the family, and Sandi, the angriest of the sisters, makes the phone call.

Yo's cousin, Lucinda, experiences an anagnorisis when her poem wins a literary prize. At that point Lucinda discovers that she "[has] a brain" (45). However, her awakening occurs just as she is about to graduate from high school. Lucinda is well aware that she has to return to the Dominican Republic because women of her culture, back then, did not attend college. She does, though, win a reprieve when the school's headmaster convinces her father to allow her to attend college for two years.

A college education would guarantee a great measure of independence for Lucinda. This makes the consequences of Yo's "betrayal" seem even more tragic. The writer kills all chances for Lucinda to reach her intellectual potential through a university education. In this context, the anagnorisis accentuates her loss.

Sara, the maid's daughter, also experiences a moment of truth. This takes place after Sara steals Yo's report. That evening, Primitiva asks her daughter what would make her life a happy one. Sara answers that her wish is for her grandmother and mother to live well, to not work so hard. In response, Primitiva tells her to devote herself to school so that one day she can help them escape from a life of poverty. At that precise moment Sara experiences her anagnorisis. She realizes that the best means to help her family is through an education in the United States. With this discovery, however, also comes the realization that her theft may have ruined the family's chances. Sara fears now that she will be sent back to the island. Fortunately for her, Yo doesn't overreact to the theft—although it creates a gulf in their relationship. And, sadly, as the reader learns in a later chapter, Primitiva dies before she can fully enjoy her daughter's success.

Yo's teacher and mentor, Professor Jordan Garfield, also experiences several anagnorises. The first one occurs, suitably, after a performance of an Oscar Wilde play. Here, Alvarez superimposes Professor Garfield's acceptance of his homosexuality on the most noted theater piece by the controversial Dubliner. "The importance of being honest," Alvarez writes (82). Later, the professor's lover, Timothy Matthews, awakens him to the sobering reality that he is dying "a slow, painful death," metaphorically, by teaching at Commodore, a small private liberal arts college. Matthews's hurtful comment leads to the couple's estrangement. When Yo returns for yet another letter of recommendation, she asks her mentor if he thinks she should divorce her second husband. Professor Garfield's counsel is that she follow her heart. He then awakens to the need to listen to his own advice, and he reconciles with his lover. This chapter concludes with the anagnorisis that supersedes all others. After Matthews' death, Yolanda visits her mentor with another of her seemingly endless requests for letters of recommendation. During her visit, she almost knocks over the urn containing Matthews' ashes. The near accident awakens Jordan Garfield to the realization that he must let go of his stodginess in order to begin living life more creatively. He commands his pupil to become a writer, rather than an academician. He then releases Matthews' ashes and in the process releases himself from his grief and from his stoicism in order to live a full life.

"The Stranger" represents an interesting break from the traditional anagnorisis. The chapter literally begins with Consuelo's awakening. Consuelo has been very concerned over the abusive relationship in which her daughter, Ruth, finds herself. Consuelo's awakening, though, rather than completing her anagnorisis, interrupts it, rendering it incomplete. In her dream, Consuelo had discovered exactly what she wanted to say in response to her daughter's dilemma. However, when Consuelo wakes up suddenly, her anagnorisis eludes her, remaining slightly out of her grasp. In her dream she had been eloquent, wise. But now she feels that she has lost the sage counsel she was offering in the dream. Searching for her lost anagnorisis, Consuelo turns to María, the village medium. María sends Consuelo to Yo so that she can dictate a letter for her daughter. The advice Consuelo dictates is the opposite of what she had dreamed. She recommends that Ruth, her daughter, honor and be submissive to her "husband"—advice that is culturally ingrained. Yo, however, as scribe, refuses to write down Consuelo's words. Instead, the scribe takes control of the letter. As Yo reads aloud what she is writing, Consuelo experiences her anagnorisis. This time it is complete, unbroken. The counsel that Yo offers Ruth picks up where Consuelo's dream left off. The advice to be strong, become independent, and to seek help are the same words Consuelo had expressed in her dream, they are the words of her anagnorisis.

The wife of Don Mundín's caretaker, María, also experiences several anagnorises. Grief-stricken and bitter over the drowning death of her son, María has shut herself off both from the world of the living and of the dead. The spirits of saints who used to "mount" her, no longer come calling. A medium, she has tried to communicate with her son to ascertain if he has safely made the crossing into the next world. However, all she hears now is silence. María's spiritual gifts have abandoned her. When Yo arrives for a writing retreat on the scene of the tragedy, María refuses to meet the new tenant. In her grief, she holds Yo's wealthy relatives responsible for the boy's death. But María's emotional isolation is hurting her family as well. A comment from her sister-in-law, regarding Sergio's increasing dependency on alcohol, awakens María to the need to set aside her bitterness in order to help her husband and children with their own pain. Her transformation is immediate, even her sexuality reemerges. The anagnorisis allows María to accept Yo's dinner invitation, for she had been avoiding the site of the tragedy. Visiting the house for the first time since her son's death, María walks through the building to see what changes the new tenant has made. The chapter concludes with the superseding anagnorisis when, after María reaches the top floor, she hears her son's voice playfully letting her know that he has arrived safely to the other side.

Tammy Rosen, Yo's best friend, experiences an anagnorisis as well. Recently divorced and recovering from an abusive marriage, Tammy believes that she is making up for lost time by sleeping with three different men. She is proud of her newfound sexuality; for once she is "popular with guys" (141). Yo accepts her friend's behavior without comment. However, when Tammy reacts angrily because she fears that Yo's omissions are fueling the rumor that the women are gay lovers, Yolanda gently confronts her with the truth. Tammy tearfully recognizes that she is trying to fill an emotional void through the meaningless relationships. At this point, she awakens to her need to become happy on her own—and her healing from the past begins in earnest.

Perhaps the most dramatic example of an anagnorisis in ¡Yo! occurs with Marie, Yo's landlady. Poor, barely educated, and extremely overweight, Marie is trapped in an abusive marriage. Her husband, Clair, beats her and openly has relationships with other women. Like in the case of her best friend Tammy, Yo gently tries to get Marie to face the truth. When Marie is on the verge of awakening, Yo reaches out to hold her. However, Clair's abrupt return home interrupts the anagnorisis. Later, though, superimposed on Yo's loss of her writings, Marie realizes that she needs to leave Clair. Yo's dramatic loss triggers Marie's decision. In spite of all this, Marie requires another push. This happens when Yo informs her that Clair has been molesting their daughter. Marie, then, with Yo's help, throws all of his possessions out of the house. Her anagnorisis is complete. In this manner, the reader sees how Alvarez dramatizes the crucial moments in the lives of her characters via their anagnorises.

THEMATIC ISSUES

Never has Alvarez explored such a wide range of issues as in ¡Yo!. The ease with which one reads the novel, as well as its bountiful humor, belies the Dominican-American's thoughtful look into the human experience. By way of her characters, Alvarez probes deeply into issues that emanate from her unique outlook on life.

Foremost among the themes examined in *¡Yo!* is the art of storytelling. Alvarez's characters fervently desire to have their stories heard. Furthermore, they want to control the storytelling process; they want their versions to reign, foregoing Yo's intervention. The family resents how Yo talks about them as if they were made-up characters. Yo's need to tell stories has deeply affected their lives. For instance, Fifi now can't read a book without wondering what the author's family thinks about it. Sandi considers herself a "fictionally victimized sister" (6). When Sandi informs Fifi that she is pregnant, she tells her to keep the news from Yo because she doesn't want her baby to become "fictional fodder" (7). In spite of their anger towards Yo, however, they can still laugh at the role that storytelling plays in the García family. This is evidenced when the mother tells her version of the convent story. In good humor, Fifi reflects how she doesn't know what the truth is any longer with regard to her family's history.

Many of the characters in *¡Yo!* become consciously involved in the storytelling process. For instance, Laura, the mother, uses her inventiveness to extricate herself from a difficult situation when the school social worker investigates Yo's background. Sara, the maid's daughter, although not a storyteller herself, allows a story of mystery and glamour to develop around her. Dexter, the suitor, elaborates, albeit awkwardly, on Yo's invention of his reporter persona. The stalker, throughout his twenty-five year obsession with Yo, only wants for her to listen to the story of his life. His need to tell his version of things, not unlike other characters, represents a release from pain and, hopefully, a return to sanity.

In *¡Yo!* two storytellers stand out above the rest. The first one is Lou Castellucci, Yo's student. He is an athletic hero who, over his interest in Penny Ross, discovers during his senior year in college that he actually enjoys studying literature. As a result, Lou enrolls in Yo's creative writing class. Initially his writings are poor imitations of television and movie plots. Yo urges him to write from his own experience. In this manner Lou's writings begin to move from fiction to truth. With each self-revealing story, Lou earns greater praise from his teacher and classmates. The act of writing opens new horizons for Lou, and along the way he learns that writing is what saves Yo. Five years later, Lou discovers that Yo has plagiarized one of his stories. At first, the theft angers him. He

is determined to denounce his former teacher. However, Lou soon realizes that what is really important is that something he created will live
on in print, even though he is denied the credit. As Lou takes great
pleasure in Penny's reaction to the story, he suddenly understands that
he created something universal, something everyone can relate to. He
also recognizes that he would have never done so without Yo's expertise.
The pressure Yo is under to earn tenure becomes the mechanism through
which her former student can forgive her. Amazingly, Yo, who is noto-
rious for stealing incidents from other people's lives, this time steals an
entire narrative—literally. As the reader observes, Yo is capable of crim-
inal behavior for a story.

The second accomplished storyteller is Yo's father. In the midst of Yo's
crisis regarding the question of motherhood, he decides to bestow a
blessing upon her. The father hopes that by doing so she can come to
terms with her decision to remain childless. However, in the case of Yo,
he decides that the blessing needs to be in the form of a story. This, he
asserts, is the only way in which his daughter will believe it. The story
he chooses to tell is a painful one, one that has caused him great shame
over the years. It revolves around the time he beat Yo, ordering her never
to tell stories again. However, in the blessing, employing a trick he has
learned from Yo, he changes the ending of the story. In this revised
version, instead of holding a belt in his hand, he holds an open hand
over Yo's head to impart a blessing. The father asks Yo to continue telling
stories, for they are what will assure the family's immortality. Thus, as
often is the case in Alvarez's third novel, storytelling redeems the storyteller.

Another theme Alvarez explores is the profound and conflictive class
differences that characterize Latin American society. In most of the
Spanish-speaking world, socioeconomic discrimination constitutes an endemic and pernicious problem. The ruling classes in Latin America have,
historically and at present, imposed their will upon the poor. In every
way, the rich consider themselves superior to those less fortunate. In
¡Yo!, the Dominican-American writer examines this issue mostly through
Sara, the maid's daughter. In spite of her considerable achievements,
Sara will always belong to the lower class in the eyes of her fellow Dominicans—particularly in the eyes of the de la Torre clan. Since childhood, she has experienced this form of socioeconomic discrimination. In
her boarding school, students were judged on the basis of whether their
father recognized them or not. As the daughter of an unknown father

and a maid, Sara finds herself at the bottom of the totem pole. Once she moves to the United States, though, the García sisters accept her as an equal. However, Sara believes that she is merely a "goodwill project" to them (57). Her mother's statement, "Those García girls! Don't you ever think you are one of them," can be read on several levels (58). First of all it can mean that Sara shouldn't acquire the habit of questioning Primitiva's parental authority. But, second, it warns Sara to remember her place in Dominican society—to squelch any aspirations she may have of crossing the rigidly drawn lines of social class. The mother confirms this when she tells her daughter that they cannot give themselves airs by requesting that Sara be sent to the same Catholic school the García sisters attended. As a result of this, the maid's daughter grows up painfully aware of being discriminated against because of her social class.

In fact, the tone of Sara's narrative is one of resentment. She resents that her mother is called by her nickname, Primitiva, rather than by her legitimate name, María Trinidad. Sara also resents that her mother looks ten years older than Laura, even though the two women are the same age. In Sara's narrative, the Garcías hold considerable power over her and her mother—although much of it is only in their minds. These sentiments, however, are based on the painfully real class struggles of everyday life in Latin America. When Yo visits Sara at the clinic, the now successful physician is still very resentful, and this makes her confrontational. She takes great pleasure in her success, as opposed to Yo's struggles. Even though Yo came in search of reconciliation, Sara remains cold, aloof, and distant. When Yo leaves the clinic, Sara predicts that she will never see any of the Garcías again.

Sara, though, alone and without family, accepts the invitation to attend Yo's wedding. She knows that she will have to face the de la Torre family, who, no matter what she achieves in life, will always see her as the maid's daughter. Also, it will be the first time that she faces them since her mother revealed the identity of Sara's father. The tone of Sara's narrative remains bitter. This is evident when she describes the awkwardness of the Garcías when they introduce her to other guests. In addition, she resents how she operates on "uncles" who, if they knew her true identity, would turn around and deny any bloodties. Furthermore, she considers "crap" what Yo says about her being one of the García girls. However, she sorrowfully acknowledges that the Garcías are the closest thing she has to a family. Still, although the Garcías and Sara are from the same country, their worlds are very different. The

García sisters have had less struggles to contend with. Sara bitterly observes that the sisters are simply caught between cultures, while she is also caught between classes.

Alvarez allows her readers to examine the other side of the coin. Yo's Tía Flor, the wife of Sara's biological father, recognizes Primitiva's daughter as one of the wedding guests. At first she takes pleasure in thinking how the maid's daughter outdid the García sisters, professionally speaking. In an imaginary conversation with Sara, Tía Flor tells her how Primitiva had worked many years for her, and that she had been very kind to the maid. However, as her thoughts progress, Tía Flor becomes increasingly hostile toward Primitiva and Sara. She labels as preposterous Primitiva's claim that her deceased husband fathered Sara. She calls Primitiva ungrateful, considering all the de la Torre family had done for her. In the end, however, Tía Flor admits the likelihood of Sara's origins. Still, she cannot set aside her class prejudices. She states that Sara is no relation to her and that, in the end, she'll always remain the maid's daughter.

María, the caretaker's wife, constitutes another case study of the conflict between social classes. She is resentful toward her husband's wealthy employers. The origins of her bitterness stem from her son's accidental drowning. The narrative states that the boy fell into the "steep dropoff," the social gap, between the rich and the poor (122). Sergio, María's husband, believes that the money of the rich protects them from the sorrow of others. After Doña Gabriela, the employer, gives María money for the boy's funeral, the caretaker's wife spits on the ground where the wealthy woman had stood. In short, the bitterness between classes is amply evident in Alvarez's novel.

Yo, however, with her comportment, eradicates the barriers between social classes. Having become totally "Americanized," she does not subscribe to Latin America's socioeconomic prejudices. Yo is egalitarian, in the truest sense of the word. She treats everyone as an equal. This is evident during her writing retreats in the Dominican Republic. The impoverished Dominican villagers repeatedly state that Yo is different from the other rich women they know. In fact, the poor, unaccustomed to wealthy people who are kind, consider Yo eccentric. She engages them in conversation. Yo also objects, time after time, to the customary phrase "You're the one who knows." Both the ruling class and the poor have become immune over the centuries to the subservience implicit in this expression. Yo, though, visibly recoils every time she hears it. Her egalitarianism does not tolerate one group's dominance over another. In fact,

Yo prepares a dinner for the caretakers and their families, something unheard of in Dominican society. But as a result, she wins over even the hardened María.

In a theme closely related to class difference, Alvarez explores poverty. José, the night watchman, offers the best example of Alvarez's approach to this theme. He has many mouths to feed, but his illiteracy diminishes his employment opportunities. José learns that he will be evicted from the lands that his family has squatted on for generations. He worries about the big changes that face his family. In desperation, he asks Yo for employment. She hires him, paying him more in one week as a night watchman than he makes in a month as a farmer. When José discovers that Yo yearns for a child, he offers his soon-to-be born child for adoption so that his offspring can later return to the island to save the family from poverty. In his mind, life in the United States is synonymous with un- limited wealth. In the following chapter, José's telephone calls to the United States, as well as his marriage proposal to Doug's daughter, alarms Yo's third husband. The reader learns how desperate many Do- minicans are to flee from poverty. In the end, though, Doug assures Yo and his daughter that they will buy land on the island. In this manner they will employ José and he will be able to better support his family.

The themes of acculturation, assimilation, cultural differences, and cul- tural displacement, are also explored in *¡Yo!*, but to a lesser degree than in *How the García Girls Lost Their Accents*. The mother's story of the early months in the Garcías' adoptive homeland illustrates a time of hardships, tensions, and fears. Each family member lost something important when they left their homeland. In addition, as is the case with every immigrant, they encountered considerable challenges while adjusting to their new lives. Sara, the maid's daughter, at first sees the United States as a prison. Here, she thinks, everyone locks themselves in their apartments, refusing even to speak with their neighbors. She also believes that living in the United States robs an immigrant of his or her identity. Specifically, Sara thinks that the García girls are extremely unsure, culturally speaking, of who they really are. In support of Sara's claim, Doug observes how his wife, Yo, has difficulty readjusting to life in the United States after her Dominican writing retreats. Even well into adulthood, Yo does not travel with ease between cultures, as Dexter Hayes, the suitor, also notes.

Part of the difficulty in adapting to change can be attributed to the cultural displacement the characters experience. Alvarez explores this theme most closely through Dexter Hayes. When Dexter informs his lover that he wants to visit her in the Dominican Republic, she strenuously objects. Her grounds: his cultural displacement would be too great. Dexter is aware that the cultural gap between them is considerable. In fact, he has labeled her a "complicated spic chick" (192). Although Dexter is aware that Yo herself experiences considerable culture shock upon her return, he still insists on making the trip. Completely out of his element, Dexter's cultural displacement is evident from the moment he arrives. He soon learns that everything on the island is an illusion, like in the Latin American novels of magical realism. Yo forbids him from showing signs of affection in public. Appearances, she informs him, are of utmost importance. So is the need to protect the virtue of Dominican women. Every time that Dexter attempts to sneak into Yo's quarters, uncles and cousins ably intercept him. Yo's suitor realizes that he is far from being competitive in this illusory world. Soon Dexter surrenders: he gives up on all pretenses by giving his tape deck to the chauffeur and the "pimp" shirt to the gardener. He is now fully convinced that he is out of his element. To aggravate matters, he makes a joke about Yo's uncle that constitutes a frontal attack upon her cultural sensibilities. As a consequence, their relationship comes to a screeching halt. The lovers realize that they are a complete cultural mismatch; that they cannot overcome his cultural displacement.

As in *How the García Girls Lost Their Accents*, Alvarez explores the theme of machismo, but once again to a lesser degree. In essence, machismo connotes a man's strength, bravery, power, and importance. These qualities are viewed as the core of the ideal man within a patriarchal society, such as Latin America. Women are primarily relegated to traditional roles in childrearing and in the maintenance of the homefront. A man perceives that he has the authority to make decisions for the women who live under his roof. In a society characterized by machismo, men attempt to control women's behavior. This includes silencing their voices. Ironically, most women in a patriarchal society accept these macho codes with few questions. The traditional roles each sex plays have been ingrained in their psyche. Lucinda, Yo's cousin, readily acknowledges that women from her culture have been taught to place greater emphasis on appearances and material well-being rather than on their growth as people. Lucinda's opportunity to attend college in the United States is ruined, not necessarily by Yo's journal, but rather by the machismo inherent in her culture. Dominican women of her generation, simply put, did not attend college. The world of higher education was restricted to men only.

Men's dominance over women is also exhibited in the case of Ruth.

When Yo writes Consuelo's reply to her daughter, the reader learns that Ruth's "husband" dominates her through fear, intimidation, and violence. He rejects Ruth's pleas for a divorce by threatening to turn her in to U.S. immigration authorities. In spite of the obvious mistreatment of her daughter, Consuelo's initial advice is for Ruth to remain obedient to her husband, to honor him and the holy banns of marriage. The mother has been culturally programmed to accept women's subservience to men. In a critique of the role that religion has played in supporting Latin America's patriarchy, the narrative states that Consuelo has learned this traditional worldview from her parish priest.

Also under the codes of machismo, men's sexual escapades are tolerated and even glorified. Both Sara and Ruth are the result of a wealthy man's forced "affair" with maids. But the pride a man receives from his sexual conquests also extends into the world of the poor. José, the night watchman, is particularly proud as well as cognizant of his prowess with women. At an early age he became experienced in sexual matters. In fact, when he learns that Yo desires a child, he misinterprets her wishes. He believes that she is requesting his help, and he subtly offers to father the child.

Dominican men, in their minds, excel in their manliness, rating far above other ethnicities and nationalities. They believe in their superiority as lovers, particularly over American men of white European descent. Both Sergio and José agree that Yo is sexually frustrated because she is married to such an American. They hold it as common knowledge that these men can't satisfy their women. This belief is reinforced when they equate Doug's vasectomy with a castration. Therefore, these Dominican characters are absolutely certain that what Yo needs in her life is a whole, functional male—like themselves.

Under the strict codes of machismo, men are possessive of the women under their protectorate. As in Alvarez's first novel, Carlos, the father, is ridiculously protective of his daughters. Sara recalls that he once challenged one of Yo's callers to a duel. Later, after Yo marries Sky Dancer, Carlos visits her college to confront the dean for allowing the marriage to take place. For the administrator's benefit, he goes as far as to dramatically pronounce his daughter dead. At the graduation ceremony, Yo's father engages in a shouting match with Sky Dancer, hurling curses at him in Spanish before a large crowd. Even after Yo has been twice married, Dexter, the suitor, has to pretend that Carlos incorrectly dialed the number of a pizza parlor to cover up his relationship with Yo. The father of the García sisters plays the role of the possessive male to the extreme. Possessiveness, however, is not a trait exclusive to Latin American males. Doug, the third husband, becomes upset by Dexter's presence at the wedding. He considers punching Yo's former suitor in the face. Later, he becomes alarmed by the night watchman's presence in the lives of his wife and daughter. Although José's marriage proposal to Corey is ridiculous, Doug takes it seriously. When José calls while only Doug is home, the husband, operating by the rigid codes of machismo, intimidates the Dominican into never calling again.

At its worst, machismo can be abusive. The reader observes this in the case of Ruth, whose "husband" tries to keep her under his dominance through beatings and threats. Ruth's own mother, Consuelo, recalls the beatings she received from her father whenever she, as a little girl, wasted time trying to learn her letters—a knowledge then deemed unsuitable for women. However, the most startling instance of spousal abuse is the case of Marie, Yo's landlady. Clair is an unfaithful and abusive husband. However, Marie still stays with him. She behaves in ways similar to many victims of spousal abuse: she invents excuses for her mate's behavior. As a result, Marie fails to act desively until she learns, through Yo, that Claire is sexually abusing their daughter. At this point the landlady embarks on the difficult path to terminate her dependency on her husband.

Related to Yo's career as a college professor, Alvarez briefly touches upon the theme of tenure. Once a university faculty member herself, the Dominican-American writer understands the considerable pressure that college professors experience in their quest for job security. "Publish or perish," the saying goes. As a professor of creative writing, Yo is subject to such pressure, and it gets to her. She tells Marie, her landlady, that she needs a quiet place to live because she is required to write a book in order to receive tenure. Later, when Yo confides to her student, Lou Castellucci, the pressure that she finds herself under, the narrative states that she pronounces the word tenure "in the solemn voice of a diagnosis of a terminal illness" (175). The topic of tenure constitutes Alvarez's nod toward her fellow academics who, like herself, have been subjected to acting like "Hyper horses [that spring] out of their stalls when the gates [lift], giving it all they [have], to the finish line," over a period of seven years. "No wonder some of these profs [are] a little odd," the narrative states (173).

The stress caused by the Dominican Republic's volatile political situation also leads characters to behave oddly. As in *How the García Girls Lost Their Accents*, this is particularly true when it comes to Yo's parents.

The reader is obliged to recall that the García family migrated to the United States because of Rafael Trujillo's dictatorship. Political tension looms darkly over Laura's story. The mother recalls how she feared that Yo would tell someone about Carlos's hidden gun, and that the SIM would swoop down in the middle of the night to arrest the entire family. The mother also relates how the horror of Dominican politics haunted the adults in the family for years after their move to the United States. When the social worker investigates the origins of the disturbing tales that Yo tells at school, Laura adds her own stories of torture and death. To Laura's relief, the social worker determines that Dominican politics are to be held accountable for the family's dysfunction.

The father's tale, or blessing, is also weighed down by the specter of Dominican politics. The narrative shares with the reader the father's role in the revolutionary underground. It also confesses that Carlos did indeed own a gun, but he claims that he only used it for hunting. He, like his wife, is terrified of Trujillo's secret police. He is also afraid of his neighbor, General Molino, who, although fond of and kind toward the girls, is capable of terrible acts. In the end, Carlos, driven by his fears, beats his daughter. Years later, he believes that perhaps because of that unfortunate incident Yo is unhappy with her destiny as a writer.

Another theme Alvarez explores that is linked to the cultural life of the Dominican Republic is that of superstition. Beginning with the maid, Primitiva, the reader learns how she migrated to the U.S. with the help of a *santera*, or a priestess who practices a religion that merges the Catholic religion with that practiced by Africans who once belonged to the Yoruba people. The *santería* priestess had prepared a power consisting of Primitiva's ground fingernails, bits of her hair, and other secret ingredients. Primitiva sprinkled the powder in the bags of the de la Torre family members who traveled to the United States, and over the years enough of her bits and pieces collected in New York to "set up a force of attraction that finally drew the rest of her to the magic city" (54). In a separate case, still back on the island, villagers turn to María in search of answers. She has supernatural gifts. For her entire life the spirits of the saints have mounted her, taking possession of her soul. The benevolent spirits speak through her, offering solutions to peoples' everyday quandaries.

Educated characters are also subject to believe in superstitions. One night the landlady is bewildered when she discovers Yo and her best friend, Tammy, sprinkling powder around the premises to protect Yo's "space." Later, told from Doug's perspective, the narrative describes Yo's

ritual of placing saucers of spirit waters around their house, supposedly
to protect them from malevolent forces. The normally well-grounded
Doug also becomes susceptible to the islanders' spiritual beliefs. He begins to suspect that the bag of Dominican soil that Yo brought back is
cursed. Doug blames the tension he is experiencing with his wife and
daughter on the soil. Although it has already been tilled into his garden,
thus becoming impossible to retrieve, Doug refills the bag and dumps it
far from the house. In the third husband's usually rational mind, the dirt
had become the source, albeit symbolic, of his familial troubles.

Another theme ¡Yo! explores is the loss of a loved one through death.
Her characters, as in real life, have different reactions to the loss of a
loved one. For instance, Professor Jordan Garfield remains stoic after the
death of his lover. In spite of being devastated, he never displays any
signs of his pain. Still, his grief is real, as manifested by his possessiveness of Matthews's ashes. Gradually, however, he starts to recover. In
the end, Professor Garfield releases his lover's remains, and in the process he opens himself to life's possibilities.

On the other hand, María is anything but stoic in the face of her son's
drowning. She lashes out against the rich, trying to place the blame for
the tragedy squarely on their shoulders. María's anger and bitterness cut
her off from the saints that speak through her. She also distances herself
from those who most love her. It is not until her sister-in-law points out
that María's family is suffering from neglect that the grieving woman
sets aside her despair. Sergio, María's husband, deals differently with his
grief. He begins to drink in excess. He also is insistent that the pool in
which his son drowned remain empty. Yo repeatedly asks him to fill it.
Defying Dominican conventions, and thus risking his employment, he
fails to fulfill Yo's request, claiming that the filter is broken. In his grief,
Sergio resorts to a pathetic attempt at fiction—in the face of the master
herself—to keep from facing the source of his anguish.

In ¡Yo!, one character proves absolutely incapable of facing reality.
Through the stalker, Alvarez examines the theme of obsession. The story
reveals an abusive mother as the cause of the man's psychological imbalance. Fifty years old in the present of the narrative, the stalker has
spent the first half of his life obsessed with his mother, and the second
half with Yo. His mental imbalance is clearly evident to others. The clerk
at the bookstore recognizes his deranged state when he calls to ask for
information about Yo's whereabouts. He also terrifies the hotel chambermaid. Ironically, the stalker works among books, in the University of

Chicago library. Spending every working day in an environment where books are treasured, the stalker cannot contain himself when it comes to the object of his obsession. He has taken a knife to Yo's novel, mutilated it, and rearranged the order of her narratives. In this distorted manner, he tries to take control of Yo's storytelling. What makes the episode of the stalker more believable is the voice Alvarez employs for the character. The tone of the narrative is irrational, disjointed, and brimming with desperation. His thoughts are a grammatical jumble, lacking commas and periods. The only word that is capitalized is the first person singular pronoun, "I," which highlights the egotistical, self-centered nature of all obsessions. Ultimately, however, all the stalker wants is what every character in *¡Yo!* is after: to tell his or her life story without Yo's intervention. He believes that once Yo listens to the events that led to his troubled state of mind, he will have exorcised himself of all his evils. Unlike the novel's other characters, because of his evident mental imbalance, the stalker has never enjoyed the benefit of an audience, not even a friendly audience of one. In the end, he has to force Yo, and the reader, to sit down and listen.

A theme that Alvarez touches upon once again is racism. When Sara asks to be sent to a Catholic school, Yo's mother starts to say that she thought that the maid's daughter would be more comfortable in a school with black kids. However, she realizes the inappropriateness of her thoughts, and she refrains from completing the statement. Professor Garfield's prejudices emerge when he first meets Yo. He notes her Latino origins and her slight accent. He thus concludes that she would be incapable of comprehending the readings and that her essays for the class would be dreadfully written. Therefore, he is thoroughly surprised with her passionate, insightful, and exhaustive work. Marie, the landlady, constitutes the novel's most racially prejudiced character. Her lack of education, as well as her low socio-economic status, is the primary factor behind her narrow view of the world. At one point or another, she strikes out against foreigners, immigrants, boatpeople, and Japanese-manufactured automobiles. Her husband, Clair, joins in with his misgivings about foreign lesbians. The stalker is also racially prejudiced. His racism is ironic considering his obsession with Yo, a Latina. He comments derisively on the racial and ethnic makeup of the hotel desk clerk. He delights in calling him a "black spic, a spic and spade (hahaha)" (281). Furthermore, he takes great pleasure in terrorizing the hotel chambermaid in large part because of her Asian origins. Although the racism in

Alvarez's third novel is not pernicious, as it is at times in *How the García Girls Lost Their Accents*, the Dominican American presents it as a considerable flaw in the constitution of her characters.

The final theme Alvarez broaches is that of motherhood; or rather, a woman's choice to remain childless. Yo agonizes over this. The issue of childlessness serves as the springboard for the novel's concluding chapter. Yo's decision not to have children is what motivates the father's blessing, which in turn is bestowed in the form of a story. He tries to console his daughter, telling her that he is proud of her accomplishments, and that in his eyes her books are his grandbabies. Interestingly, it is a choice that Julia Alvarez herself has had to make. She candidly writes about this issue in the essay "Imagining Motherhood," which appears in *Something to Declare*. Furthermore, the reader will find that the Dominican American reflects on virtually all of the issues that inform her writing in this interesting collection of essays.

A READER RESPONSE READING OF *¡YO!*

A reader's background knowledge plays a vital role in the act of reading. The role of background knowledge in reading is best explained by schema theory. Schema theory postulates that we employ items that are familiar to us, our internal model of the world, in order to interpret new concepts that arise from an emerging situation with which we are unfamiliar. Furthermore, the interaction between the unfamiliar sequence of events and our internal model of the world is what guides our behavior in that situation. A schema is, therefore, the framework within which we perceive and interpret the world.

Reader-centered theories have appropriated the fundamentals of schema theory in order to explain more fully the role of a reader's background knowledge in extracting meaning from the text. Reader-centered theorists maintain that any written text does not carry meaning by itself. A text merely provides directions for readers as to how they should retrieve or construct meaning from their own, previously acquired knowledge or schemata. In reader-centered theories, the comprehension of a text is an interactive process between the reader's background and the text. In order to attain efficient comprehension, it is required that the reader be able to relate the textual material to his or her own knowledge.

The reader brings to the literary work a background knowledge that interacts with the directions provided by the written word. The expectations of the reader will either be confirmed or modified by the information acquired through the reading process. As the parts of the puzzle, so to speak, fall into place, an illusory world is created in the reader's mind. The process of reading, however, is not a linear affair, nor is it cumulative: the initial assumptions of the reader generate a frame of reference that assists in the interpretation of the text. What comes next in the narrative may transform, retrospectively, the reader's original understanding. As the reader progresses in his or her activity, he or she sheds assumptions, revises beliefs, makes more and more complex inferences and anticipations. In essence, reading takes place backwards and forwards, and at times simultaneously, predicting future events and recollecting others. The reader constantly refers back to what was read before in order to construct a coherent sense of what is to come. Reading, therefore, is a complex, multilayered activity in which backgrounds and foregrounds are constantly superimposed upon one another in order for the reader to create meaning.

Proponents of reader-centered literary theories compare the reading process to looking into a kaleidoscope. Different perspectives, expectations, and recollections revolve around one another. Every sentence contains a preview of the next, and thus it becomes a viewfinder for what is to come. However, what we read also modifies what we have already read. By means of this process, by looking into the kaleidoscope, the reader extracts meaning from the text. If the reader is successful, then he or she will have brought into being the text's "virtual dimension," in other words, its total meaning.

The interesting aspect of *¡Yo!* is that from the onset there will be two different sets of readers: those who have read *How the García Girls Lost Their Accents*, and those who have not. Thus, the readers of Alvarez's first novel will have a broader background knowledge. However, this by no means excludes those unfamiliar with the lives of the García family from understanding and enjoying the sequel. Like any well-constructed follow-up, *¡Yo!* asserts itself, acquiring a life and an identity all its own. Alvarez, a skilled writer, does not spend too much time treading over old terrain. She uses her first work merely as a springboard from which to create new characters, explore new themes, and conduct yet another experiment in the art of storytelling. The only difference is that, on occasion, readers of the first novel will delight in recognizing characters and incidents with which they are already familiar. For instance, the reader of *How the García Girls Lost Their Accents* may recognize the rationale of narrating the first chapter from Fifi's perspective. The reader of Alvarez's first novel will recall Fifi as the most level-headed of the sisters. Thus, in the midst of the family's sentiments of anger, resentment, and betrayal, Fifi is the most likely to remain reasonable. She is the best equipped to help mend the fences.

Several other characters from the first novel reemerge to have their stories told in greater depth—for instance Lucinda and Primitiva. A few other incidents and character traits reoccur, such as the mother's story of the convent, her fear that she will end up in Bellevue Hospital, and her constant threats to pour Tabasco Sauce in Yo's mouth. Even the appearance of an object, such as Yo's typewriter, will help the reader of the first novel travel back to his or her previous reading and enjoy the intertextual reference, the link between both works.

These linkages are what allow Alvarez to play with the Garcías' acute awareness of themselves as literary characters. From the narrative's first moments, the members of the García clan realize that the events of their lives have been appropriated for fiction. They now have parallel existences as made-up characters. Irritated, Fifi expresses her consternation, stating that she feels that her entire life is losing ground to fiction. She can no longer read a book without wondering what the author's family is thinking. Another sister, Sandi, considers herself a victim of fictional abuse. The mother is horrified that the family secrets have now become part of the public domain. However, not every character takes Yo's work as seriously. Most notable is Otto, Fifi's husband, whose reaction, the reader observes, indicates his belief that the family is making a mountain out of a molehill.

Still, in spite of Otto's nonchalance, the García's multiple existences are bound to astound the reader of the first novel. The characters now have a double existence: their "true" and their "fictional" selves. From being the objects of the first novel, they have now become the subjects. In essence, they have lost control over their stories. This is what really angers them. Ironically, as the reader of the first novel is well aware, Yo controlled their stories all along. But, as readers, we witness how the sisters plot to regain control of their stories. Sandi, who is pregnant, tries to block Yo's access to this evolving part of her life. At the conclusion of the chapter, when Sandi calls and begins to tell her version of her child's birth to Yo's answering machine, she successfully wrestles the position of storyteller away from Yo. From that point on, the reader encounters Yo as the subject. In other words, Yolanda García has now lost control of her story. Thus, ¡Yo!'s intertextuality, its ability to create multiple existences for the García family, makes the novel multidimensional.

What the narrative of *¡Yo!* most capitalizes on are the reader's recollections. The reader of *How the García Girls Lost Their Accents* has a slight advantage over those who have yet to read the Dominican-American's first work. He or she will be able to recall characters and incidents that reach back to the first text. However, even within *¡Yo!* there is plenty for the reader to look back upon and revise his or her assumptions about Alvarez's fictional world. Like pieces of a puzzle, the reader is obliged to frame the incoming information against his or her background knowledge in order to extract the full meaning of the text. The narrative's linkages to past events occur most notably in the chapter titled "The Wedding Guests." Numerous characters from previous chapters, as well as from the first novel, step back into the kaleidoscope. However, in addition to their character traits, they bring along with them the entire baggage of their stories. This makes it imperative for the reader to remain constantly mindful of what he or she has previously read.

The reader's recollections help provide the novel's most humorous moments. For instance, when Corey meets Dexter Hayes, she secretly denigrates his "phony" Southern accent. In return, Dexter labels Corey, Yo's soon-to-be stepdaughter, a "workout." In addition, he thinks to himself that Yo finally got the family she wanted—including a headache or two. When Lucinda recognizes Dexter, she recalls how his and Yo's ruse didn't fool anyone in the Dominican Republic. Also, regarding Lucinda, the reader observes how she is still bitter over the role Yo played in her life. The cousin scornfully wonders why Roe, the young man at the center of their rivalry, isn't among the wedding guests proclaiming Yo the true love of his life. Shortly thereafter, the reader is reminded of Dexter's fondness for Latina women when he tries to hit on Sara, the maid's daughter. Superimposed on this incident is Tía Flor's agony when she recognizes Sara as her deceased husband's illegitimate child.

"The Wedding Guests" is a masterful chapter during which the past and present of the narrative rapidly revolve around one another. In this chapter, as the reader progresses in his or her activity, he or she sheds assumptions, revises beliefs, and makes more and more complex inferences and anticipations regarding the narrative. The reader constantly refers back to what was read before in order to construct a coherent sense of what is to come. In fact, the narrative's past, its present, and the reader's future expectations spin so quickly that everything threatens to end in chaos. The characters and their individual stories seem headed on a collision course. It is precisely at this point in the narrative that Yo confides to her best friend, Tammy, her well-founded fears that things are falling apart. Tammy, from her perspective, assures Yo that things are going fine, that the tapestry of stories that she is trying to weave together is blending nicely. At this very moment, the tension caused by the clashing of stories finds a release: Dexter lets go of his balloons. The reader, as well as the characters, looks heavenward. Everyone, including the readers, lets go of his or her anxieties. The characters remember that they are there for Yo's wedding. The narrative then distances the reader even further from the tension by way of the trapped ewe. This crisis brings everyone together. Like the balloons, releasing the ewe allows the approaching chaos, the spiraling out of control of the characters' individual stories, to come to an abrupt halt. Everyone, including the reader, focuses on the defenseless animal. Then, after the ewe's release, everyone is free to climb up a hill where Yo, looking like an angel, awaits.

In the novel's final chapter, Carlos García, the family patriarch, takes center stage. Thus far he has been confined to a minor role. The readers of *How the García Girls Lost Their Accents* are well acquainted with the exiled father-physician. In this chapter, his usually explosive nature is subdued. Concerned over Yo's depression, Carlos concentrates on helping his daughter deal with her choice to remain childless. After some thought he decides to offer Yo a blessing in order to lift the curse. He chooses to bestow his blessing in the form of a story. For this purpose he selects a tale that the reader has encountered twice before: once in *How the García Girls Lost Their Accents*, seen from Yo's perspective; and again told in the second chapter of *¡Yo!*, seen this time from the mother's perspective. Consequently, the reader has the background knowledge necessary to place all the perspectives together and draw his or her own conclusions.

In the first version of the event, Yo mentions the gun episode in relation to Trujillo's secret police storming into the house in search of her father. Because of her parent's reaction to the story she told the general, she holds herself responsible for the impending arrest. However, the reader gets the impression that, later, in adulthood, Yo realizes that the incident was a result of the dangerous times Dominicans lived in. To all appearances, Yolanda García has absolved herself from guilt. Therefore, the gun episode doesn't merit more than few paragraphs in her narrative. When Laura retells the same story in *¡Yo!*, this incident acquires epic proportions. It is seen as the point where the chances for a healthy mother–daughter relationship come crashing to the ground. Laura loses, from this point forward, her ability to trust Yo, and vice versa. Told from Laura's perspective, the reader sees the incident as a rupture, as the gap through which Yo's storytelling not only hurts, but also endangers the family. The father's version of the same incident, however, rather than blaming Yo, is self-recriminating. The event has become something of a curse for him. Therefore, the tone of his blessing is confessional. Carlos holds himself responsible for Yo's depression. Although what resides at the heart of her sadness has little to do with storytelling (rather, it's a career choice), the father sees it all in terms of the rash beating he gave his child during very frightening times. Moreover, during this beating, he ordered her never again to tell stories. Therefore, seen as a whole, it is not surprising for the reader to conclude that Yo is the least trauma-tized of the three over this event. The beating had a far greater impact on the lives of the parents than on the child. Their guilt lives on, and is considerable. On the other hand, the only proof the reader needs that Yo was not greatly affected by the incident is the fact that she continues to tell stories. In essence, she has blatantly disobeyed the mandate of that night. Thus the reader finds that Yo, like her role model, Scheherazade, continues to survive and to grow through her storytelling.

6

In the Name of Salomé
(2000)

The name of Pedro Henríquez Ureña is renown among serious students of Latin American literature and culture. Although Pedro died nearly half a century ago, his scholarly essays and books are still read with reverence in graduate programs throughout the world. To a lesser degree, Pedro is recognized for his poetic talent. His younger brother, Max Henríquez Ureña, is also known for his work as a literary critic and historian. In addition, Max is remembered, somewhat infamously, for his career as a diplomat serving the regime of Rafael Trujillo. On the other hand, Salomé Ureña, their mother, the Dominican National Poet, is little known outside of her country. And only serious students of Dominican history remember Francisco Henríquez. His four-month reign as president rendered him a footnote in the legacy of U.S. intervention in Latin America. Lastly, the name of Salomé Camila Henríquez Ureña is the least known of this talented and volatile family. Most scholars of Latin American culture are unaware that the Henríquez Ureña brothers had a sister. Thus, her contribution to the family's literary and historical legacy remains largely unknown.

In 2000, Algonquin Books of Chapel Hill published Julia Alvarez's fourth novel, *In the Name of Salomé*. The saga of the Henríquez Ureña family represents her second sally into the realm of the historical novel. *In the Name of Salomé* also represents her most ambitious work to date. Alvarez chose to write about a Dominican family whose members were well known in their lifetimes. However, in comparison, their existences lack the poignancy, the pathos, and the heart-wrenching drama of the lives of the Mirabal sisters. Furthermore, in a direct challenge to her skills as a writer, Alvarez selects Salomé Camila Henríquez Ureña to serve as the novel's primary focal point. In essence, she chooses the character who, on the surface, is the least remarkable, the least interesting of any of the Henríquez Ureñas. In spite of these odds, Alvarez produces yet another remarkable work. What the reader encounters in this novel is a writer at the peak of her trade. *In the Name of Salomé* is bolder, more adventurous, and more experimental than anything the Dominican-American has written before. Perhaps as a consequence of this distinction it has received more mixed reviews than any of Alvarez's other novels. Still, the reader identifies with the life struggles of Salomé and Camila. Their stories stand as a testament to women of talent, vision, and strength.

In the "Acknowledgements" section of *In the Name of Salomé*, Alvarez recalls how the Dominican writer Chiqui Vicioso imposed the subject of the Henríquez Ureña family upon her. As Vicioso handed Alvarez the Henríquez Ureña *Epistolario*, as well as an anthology of Salomé's poems, she pronounced: " 'Your next book, Julia!' " (356). Alvarez could not refuse such a mandate. She immediately immersed herself in the lives and times of her subjects. Alvarez even traveled to Cuba in October of 1997 to research the life that Salomé Camila Henríquez Ureña led there. The result of her efforts is a novel where love, literature, history, political intrigue, the reverence for one's country, and the desire for self-determination—individual and national—converge in a portrait of this notable Dominican family and the times in which they lived.

PLOT DEVELOPMENT AND STRUCTURE

As in the case of Julia Alvarez's first novel, *How the García Girls Lost Their Accents*, the reader who desires a neat, linear plot will be challenged by the structure of *In the Name of Salomé*. However, while *How the García Girls Lost Their Accents* constitutes the work of the writer at the beginning of her novelistic career, *In the Name of Salomé* represents the writer at her apex. Alvarez exhibits complete mastery over the plan, design, scheme, and patterns in this work of fiction. *In the Name of Salomé* has an underlying structure that demonstrates that the author is in control of the story, and that any event she is telling will eventually make sense. In spite of being an experimental novel in its structure, the plot is well constructed. Although Alvarez's work disregards the traditional, linear, and easily discernible plot, in the end the patient reader will find that the journey was well worth the effort.

Since *In the Name of Salomé* is, indeed, an experimental novel, the reader may at times become frustrated with the structure. *In the Name of Salomé* consists of a Prologue, sixteen chapters, and an Epilogue. Eight of the chapters correspond to Salomé's story; the other eight correspond to Camila's. The chapters are alternately dedicated to the stories of each of the central characters. However, Alvarez's novel moves unconventionally in time: the chapters narrating Salomé's life move forward; the chapters dealing with Camila's life move backwards. For instance, Salomé's story begins with her earliest memories and move forward until her death. On the other hand, Camila's story begins in the Prologue, as she prepares to return to Cuba. She has just retired from a successful career as a college professor in the United States. Beginning at this advanced point in Camila's life, the narrative moves in reverse order, ending with her earliest memories. The titles of the chapters are borrowed from the titles of poems written by Salomé Ureña. The chapters with Spanish titles correspond to her story, while the chapters with the same titles translated into English narrate Camila's life. The chapter titles, like the narrative, move in opposite directions, intersecting precisely in the middle as one moves closer to death and the other moves closer to birth.

The novel is divided symmetrically: two parts, consisting of eight chapters each. Because the stories move in opposite directions, the separate plots meet in the end. In the Epilogue, the reader learns that Camila has been telling both stories all along. She made the stories run parallel to one another in order to give meaning to her own life: "I learned her story. I put it side by side with my own. I wove our two lives together as strong as rope and with it I pulled myself out of the pit of depression and self-doubt" (335). Indeed, at the conclusion of the novel, Camila at last addresses the reader directly by employing the first-person perspective. That is because when the reader initially meets her she is insecure, indecisive. The reader needs to travel backwards to understand the causes of her depression and self-doubt. The Epilogue, however, presents a transformed Camila. She is now a strong, assured character that is in control of her destiny.

As many writers of Hispanic origin do when telling a family saga, Alvarez employs a tree to help orient the reader. Structurally, the Dominican-American writer experiments with regard to the location of the family tree. Rather than appearing prior to the beginning of the narrative—as tradition dictates—the family tree appears at the conclusion of the Prologue. The unusual placement of the tree coincides with Camila giving her assistant, Nancy Palmer, a condensed version of the family history. Thus, by the beginning of the first chapter, the reader is already familiar with the framework of the entire story, and the remainder of the narrative serves to flesh it out.

In the Name of Salomé deals with the personal histories of Salomé Ureña and Salomé Camila Henríquez Ureña. Since their stories span from 1850 through 1973, Alvarez is faced with the challenge of situating the reader with regard to time. To achieve this, under each chapter title are the location and the dates in which the events take place. However, the Dominican-American strategically places historical events within the narrative to help the reader relive the spirit of the times. For instance, woven within the story of the Henríquez Ureña family are Lincoln's assassination, the U.S. centennial celebrations, Alexander Graham Bell's invention of the telephone, President Garfield's assassination, Prohibition, World War I, the Soviet Union's development of the atom bomb, McCarthyism, and the Cuban Revolution. In this manner, the reader can grasp how the lives of the Henríquez Ureñas span across events that impacted several generations of Americans. In addition, this simple device makes the existence of this Dominican family seem truly international.

POINT OF VIEW

The manner in which Alvarez employs the point of view in her fourth novel helps bring the characters to life. The reader can virtually hear the voices of Salomé Ureña and Salomé Camila Henríquez Ureña as they share their lives with us. The Dominican-American's choice of vantage points gives the story an immediacy that helps the reader identify with the central characters in their struggles as women and artists.

A point of view constitutes—in the most basic sense—the position of the narrator in relation to her story. It is the outlook from which events are related. In Alvarez's work, each chapter alternates between the points of view of Salomé and Camila. The chapters with the titles in Spanish are told from Salomé's perspective. Salomé's viewpoint is that of the first-person limited. The chapters with the titles in English are told from Camila's perspective. Camila's viewpoint is that of the third-person limited. However, in the Epilogue of *In the Name of Salomé*, Camila switches to the first-person. This change coincides with the character having finally come to terms with her existence. Thus, in the end, Camila is in control of the story of her life.

As usual, Alvarez employs several innovative devices that make her use of the points of view more interesting. For instance, in the Prologue, Camila tries to explain to Marion why she wants to return to Cuba. By way of explanation she begins to tell Salomé's story. Marion objects to this beginning, arguing that she wants to learn more about Camila. This sets the stage for Camila to insist that her story begins with the story of her mother, for their stories are entwined. In this manner, the reader has the motive behind the narrative: Camila must tell the story of the entire Henríquez Ureña family in order to understand her own.

As in each of her previous novels, Alvarez once again employs the device of the medium in order to rescue the viewpoints of the distant past and effectively translate them into the present. However, she has never accomplished this more discreetly and effectively than in this novel. A medium is an individual with the ability to communicate with the dead. In this case, it is Camila herself who possesses this skill. As Camila tells her assistant, Nancy, of the family history, the narrative becomes explicit about her role as the medium: "Just introducing these ghosts by name has recalled them so vividly, they rise up before her. . . . Maybe it is a good thing to finally face each one squarely. Maybe that is the only way to exorcise ghosts. To become them" (42). By becoming one of the ghosts, Camila is able to help the reader understand the meaning behind the family mementos found in a box: a small flag on a broken stick, baby teeth, Nísidas's poems, and a catechism book. At the conclusion of the novel, to the reader's surprise, Camila has been telling her story, as well as her mother's, from beyond the grave. Camila has been a ghost all along. Blinded by cataracts at the end of her days, Camila traces her gravestone with her fingers, and she recognizes that all the details are correct, particularly the date of her death. This constitutes a feat impossible to accomplish without the benefit of a second medium, which for the first time in any of her novels, is the author herself.

In addition to her use of the medium, Alvarez resorts to other devices to make the characters' viewpoints seem immediate. Chapter Six, "Ruinas," told from Salomé's viewpoint, consists of the letters the poet writes to her husband while he studies in France. These missives reflect the pain of separation, loneliness, and, ultimately, betrayal. By employing this device to convey Salomé's vantage point, the reader is able to share the intensity of the character's feelings. Earlier in the novel, Chapter Five,

"Love and Yearning," told from Camila's point of view, is built upon a series of unsent letters written to Marion. These letters move the plot forward in a swift manner. However, the letters also serve an emotional purpose. Because Camila has postponed her sentimental and personal development to help her father in his hopeless quest to regain the presidency of his country, she writes these unsent letters to extract meaning from her sacrifice. Thus, the use of this device to convey the central character's viewpoint serves as a catharsis for both Camila and the reader.

A last feature of Alvarez's use of point of view arises from the trajectory of the story with regard to time. Salomé's story moves forward beginning with her childhood. It continues progressing in chronological order until her death. On the other hand, Camila's story moves backward in time. With regard to Alvarez's use of the point of view, the daughter's story is more interesting. The Prologue begins as Camila prepares to return to Cuba. She is a mature, retired woman, who is still searching for her place in the world. From here Camila's story moves backward until, in the last chapter, she relates her story through the eyes of a three-year-old child. Immediately afterwards, in the Epilogue, the reader encounters Camila as a woman who has returned to her country of birth to await her death. However, far from being sad and pessimistic, the vantage point of the elderly Camila constitutes the viewpoint of a victor. The reader finds that, at last, Camila has gained a strong sense of self. She finally is at peace with the role she has played in life, and she is content with her niche in the family's extraordinary history.

CHARACTER DEVELOPMENT

Camila Henríquez Ureña represents Julia Alvarez's greatest challenge so far in developing a well-rounded character, particularly with respect to creating a character that will hold the reader's interest. Camila lacks Yolanda García's willfulness. She also lacks the strength and determination of Minerva, or Dedé, Mirabal. In fact, Camila suffers from a severe identity crisis. The dominant figures of her family overwhelm her. Compared to the other Henríquez Ureñas she is meek and out of place. So demanding are the members of her family that Camila feels that she is always at their disposal, that she never has the time to do what she wants in life. This was particularly true in the case of her father, Pancho, who "Even in death . . . makes many demands on her!" (150). Even Camila's aunts exercise considerable control over her life. Marion argues that Camila's devotion to family stifles her personal development. Beginning in childhood, family members fight to control Camila's life. Therefore, it should not surprise the reader that for the greater part of the narrative Camila suffers from an identity crisis.

To a large degree, Camila's lack of a self-concept stems from her condition of being motherless. Salomé is barely a memory in her mind. Camila has only a few precious recollections of her mother that she plays back over and over. However, what little Camila remembers about Salomé is shrouded by the pain and chaos that follows her mother's death. Furthermore, at the time, the concept of death was far beyond the grasp of the three-year-old girl. Therefore, the lack of a sympathetic female role model contributes significantly to Camila's identity crisis.

In order to establish a sense of who she is, then, Camila constantly compares her life to her mother's. More to the point, in the end, the reader discovers that Camila has placed her story side by side with her mother's so that she can better understand herself. Early in the narrative, in old age, Camila turns to her mother's poems—opening her poetic anthology at random—in order to seek answers to life's dilemmas. Her mother's legacy even impacts Camila's professional life. The year of the centennial anniversay of Salomé's birth, Camila is invited to give lectures throughout the United States. The topic: her mother's poetry. Thus, Camila's mother also makes demands from beyond the grave. However, as opposed to her father's cumbersome presence, Camila welcomes her mother's more gentle intrusions; it fills a lifelong absence. Throughout the narrative, Camila consistently looks back on her mother's life in the hope of discovering how to live her own. Sadly, though, the picture that others have created of Salomé is a fantasy. The Henríquez Ureña family, as well as the poet's compatriots, have idealized her. This idealization, then, condemns Camila to pursue an identity that doesn't exist in reality.

Because of Camila's unattainable quest to replicate her mother's image, she grows up confused and indecisive. Her low self-esteem leads to bouts of depression (and Camila grows up unaware that Salomé was subject to the same). Camila turns to other sources for comfort. Early in the narrative, the reader witnesses how Camila dulls her insecurities with a glass of wine every evening. At the same time, we learn that her doctor prescribes sedatives for her. When Camila confides in Marion that she feels worthless, Marion replies that she is incorrect. The irony resides in that Marion lists the accomplishments of other members of the Henríquez Ureña family in order to dispel the feeling of worthlessness from

Camila's mind. Thus, Marion's argument ultimately reinforces what Camila already believes about herself—that her achievements will never meet the high standards set by her family.

With Camila's story told in reverse chronological order, it is not until late in the narrative that the reader meets her as a teenager. In the Camila Henríquez Ureña of Alvarez's creation, the character is prone to the same existential angst of all adolescents. While Camila awaits the arrival of her aunt Ramona to Santiago, Cuba, her thoughts are those of an unhappy teenager. Angry with her father, she probes her recently arrived aunt for information regarding how Papancho and Tivisita came to be wed so shortly after her mother's death. Significantly, as well as typically, most of the adolescent's hostility is directed toward the intruder: her stepmother. Throughout the narrative—through words and actions—Camila exhibits her resentment toward Tivisita. However, her feelings are fraught with guilt; for she is cognizant that Tivisita has always been kind, loving, and patient with her. Moreover, Camila's guilt is compounded after she foresees her stepmother's early death. Because of the confusion between her vision and her resentment, Camila feels responsible for the tragedy. Thus, Camila's teenage experiences accentuate her isolation and her sense of worthlessness.

To aggravate matters, Camila also suffers a crisis with regard to her sexual identity. Never has the Dominican-American writer explored a character's sexuality more in depth. Moreover, this feature of Camila's characterization serves to isolate her even further from others. Camila explores heterosexuality with the sculptor, Domingo. Significantly, though, the narrative states that her attraction toward him is based on his blackness, which reminds her of her mother. Earlier, Camila had experienced romantic love with Scott Andrews. He offered her stability and the possibility of building a family of her own. She was twenty-nine at the time and her only desire was to be happy (192). However, this relationship—like the one with Domingo—came to an abrupt end. By the time it is possible for her to develop a relationship with the Spanish poet Jorge Guillén, Camila is no longer interested in relationships. She has realized that her confusion over her sexual identity only has led to pain, and she has decided to remain alone forever.

The closest thing that Camila experiences to genuine love is her relationship to Marion. A lesbian relationship seems natural to her. Camila knows this from the time she is an adolescent. A man's touch has always repulsed her. However, because of societal and cultural taboos, Camila is never allowed to explore this aspect of her character. Her homosexuality, then, becomes a terrible burden she must deal with in secret. Nevertheless, even in her relationship with Marion, Camila is overwhelmed by another character's dominance. Marion is strong, aggressive, and masculine, while in comparison Camila appears to be weak, passive, and feminine. However, Camila does assert herself, albeit quietly.

Where Camila does express herself rather openly is in her political views. During her first sojourn in Cuba, she leads other women in open defiance of Fulgencio Batista's dictatorship. Because of her opposition to Batista—which included a two-week stint in jail—she flees Cuba for the United States. In the United States, Camila pronounces at least one speech condemning Rafael Trujillo's reign. Eventually, in her most profound political statement, she swims against the political tide by moving to Cuba to offer a helping hand to Fidel Castro's communist revolution. It is here where she gives of herself most freely, and where she reconciles with her identity.

Influenced by her mother's example, as well as by the example of the other members of the Henríquez Ureña clan, Camila becomes a poet. Writing, however, is an activity that Camila conducts in secret, almost clandestinely. This is because she lacks confidence in her work—even though another Spanish poet, Juan Ramón Jiménez, encourages her to continue writing. Already in middle age, Camila fantasizes that she has finally found her place in the world. But Pedro's lack of support drives her away from creative writing for good. Again, because of her self-doubt Camila allows another opportunity to slip away.

During Camila's life in the United States she has to deal with yet another troublesome facet of her identity: her race and ethnicity. The narrative of *In the Name of Salomé* actually begins with the questions others commonly ask about Camila's origins: Is she Italian, Jewish, or black? Much later in the novel, Camila and other members of her family are denied admission to Washington, D.C. restaurants because of their skin color. While graduate students, because xenophobia found fertile ground in the United States during World War I, Camila and Pedro are discriminated against because of their foreignness. To make matters worse, even after living in the United States for many years, Camila is never completely comfortable in her adopted homeland because of her relationship with the English language. Her heavy accent distances her from others. All this, of course, serves to intensify her already severe identity crisis.

It is as a teacher where Camila most distinguishes herself. Thus, being a teacher is at the core of her identity. Toward the end of her life in the

United States, Camila realizes that what she will leave behind as her legacy are her students. Her inclination to be an educator explains why she suffers from the "teacher's handicap" (8). This handicap makes Camila place herself in the background of every event. Camila's virtual invisibility, then, reflects what has been the primary mission in her life: to tell the story of the illustrious members of her family who have passed on before her.

By the Epilogue, nevertheless, Camila has discovered her identity. Narrating the closing segment of the novel from the first-person point of view, Camila is now strong, assertive, and in control of her story. In the end, although aged, Camila is more forceful than ever. She selects her own tombstone, her grave, and refuses to be buried alongside her famous mother. At the end of her life Camila no longer feels that she should have replicated her mother's existence. Readers need to travel backwards in her story to understand the causes of her identity crisis. At the conclusion of the narrative, Camila is confident and comfortable with herself. Her work as an educator during the early years of the Cuban Revolution allow her to discover her place in the world. She is proud of the legacy she leaves behind—thousands of students who know how to read, think, and question. More importantly, Camila understands that she accomplished everything her mother would have hoped for her.

Salomé's characterization, on the other hand, revolves around her identity as a poet. At the onset of the narrative, for the benefit of her American audience, Alvarez provides an analogy that expresses the manner in which the poet is respected in her homeland: "Emily Dickinson is to the United States as Salomé Ureña is to the Dominican Republic" (3). Thus, Salomé's place as the first great woman poet of her nation is affirmed. In fact, Salomé's poetic identity is inextricably linked to the identity of the Dominican Republic. Salomé's birth and the birth of her country are superimposed upon one another. In this manner they become the same thing in the mind of the reader. In fact, what inspires Salomé to write her most remembered verses is the desire to help free the Dominican Republic from Spanish rule. Her patriotic poems find their way instantly into the hearts of her fellow Dominicans. Presidents and generals recite her verses to demonstrate their love for the island nation. Her fellow islanders turn her into an icon, a model of patriotism. However, in spite of her elevated stature in the eyes of other Dominicans, Salomé still feels the same, and looks the same. The difference resides in that after she begins to publish her poems, others treat her with respect. In a humorous passage, Salomé reflects upon how even when she talks about the weather her inane comments seem profound to others. And that is because Dominicans have elevated her to the rank of *poetisa*—the nation's muse.

Salomé's exalted stature as the national poet, however, locks her permanently into that role. Because of the powerful political identity Salomé created for herself through her verses, she cannot write poetry of a personal nature. The people closest to Salomé—her father, sister, husband, and sons—deny her this right. Her legacy is to remain the *poetisa de la patria*, the poet of the nation, for eternity. Her individual voice, in particular her voice as a woman, is silenced by the role others have assigned to her. Salomé, then, is condemned to function exclusively as spokesperson for the yearnings of a young nation.

Salomé's inclination to become a poet stems from the profound love she feels for her father, Nicolás Ureña—a poet, political activist, attorney, and member of Dominican aristocracy. She adores this man. Their relationship begins with conspiratorial underpinnings, as her parents are separated and she lives with her mother. However, in great fun, they communicate clandestinely through written verses. For this purpose they use pseudonyms: she Herminia, and he Nísidas. So profound is the influence that Nicolás exerts on Salomé's identity that she divides her life into BN and AN—Before and After Nísidas (24). Furthermore, the narrative categorizes the difference between these periods as the difference between darkness and light.

Salomé becomes so dependent upon her father for support that she falls into a two-year depression following his death. However, since childhood the national poet has a tendency toward melancholy and despair. Her predisposition toward sadness foreshadows her frail physical identity, as well her eventual death from consumption. In fact, Salomé's deteriorating health becomes an integral part of her development as a character. Furthermore, her declining physical condition reflects the worsening state of her beloved country. The young nation Salomé represents still has many generations to go to learn how to exist as a democracy.

Salomé's poor health, in addition, distances her from others, literally and metaphorically. Her acute shyness also accentuates the distance between herself and others. Like her daughter Camila, Salomé is an introvert. She finds refuge from life's hardships within herself. The more she is honored as a poet, the more she withdraws from her admirers. Salomé is portrayed as painfully shy and insecure through adolescence and young adulthood. But like Camila, she acquires a sense of self through her role as a teacher. Ultimately, Salomé becomes self-assured. During her last days she wears the tiara of *poetisa de la patria* with dignity and honor in spite of her failing health.

Salomé's desire to be loved intensifies her loneliness. Because of her looks and her African heritage, she feels that a man will never want her. Moreover, Salomé's shyness and insecurity constitute a barrier that makes it difficult for her to attract suitors. The character's self-description portrays her as unattractive and undesirable: "... Salomé, of the funny nose and big ears with hunger in her eyes and Africa in her skin and hair" (94).

Salomé's poetic talents, however, attract men to her in spite of her shyness. This is particularly true in the case of Pancho. Her poems draw him to her. Salomé's verses are like cream left out for a puppy (133). The poet ultimately realizes that if she wants to win Pancho's heart all she has to do is write. Their relationship changes her life forever. But these changes are not necessarily for the best. Salomé loses much of her spirit and independence because of Pancho's domineering character. In addition, he causes her great suffering because of his self-centeredness and infidelity.

When it appears that Salomé will completely lose her identity to Pancho's demands, she meets Eugenio Hostos, the Puerto Rican essayist and educator. He helps liberate the poet from her husband's grasp. A positivist, Hostos believes in the power of reason, progress, and science over superstition and violence. In addition, he is portrayed as a forerunner of men who support women's rights. Salomé and the positivist develop a strong mutual respect for one another. Hostos influences her greatly, convincing Salomé to become an educator.

In this manner, Salomé—like Camila after her—begins to devote her life to others. She decides to stop writing so that she can better serve her students and her family. Because of Salomé's devotion to the development of humankind in the positivist model, she sacrifices her poetic voice. However, the roles of mother and educator matter to her the most. Although the Salomé Ureña of *In the Name of Salomé* seems aware that her legacy as a poet will be lasting, she remains more proud of the children she leaves behind—in particular Pedro and Camila. She intuitively understands that the good deeds they will perform as educators will have a far more lasting impact than her poetry.

Two other characters of *In the Name of Salomé* are also worth examining: Francisco Henríquez and Pedro Henríquez Ureña. Francisco, also referred to as Pancho and Papancho, is an interesting study of virtues and defects. Pancho's admiration for Salomé's patriotic verses draws him into the narrative. But from the onset the attraction is a bit bewildering, as Salomé's older sister acknowledges. Ramona wonders how Salomé, a twenty-eight-year-old woman, can tolerate the attentions of a nineteen-year-old boy. The narrative repeatedly refers to Pancho's attraction for Salomé as puppy love. But Salomé also falls in love with the younger man, and, taking advantage of his awe for her as a poet, she writes her way into his heart.

While the narrative describes Salomé's physical appearance in less than flattering terms, Pancho is described as beautiful in youth, and as "presidential" in his later years. Indeed, his presence is commanding—physical and otherwise. Pancho has a gift for dealing with people, presiding effortlessly over gatherings, and exhibiting the confidence of a great leader. In fact, what most attracts Salomé is Pancho's ability to earn everyone's respect.

Pancho, however, is difficult to deal with because of his stubbornness. This is evident when he becomes intent on regaining the presidency of the Dominican Republic after he is ousted in a U.S.-led coup. Everyone but him believes that the cause is hopeless. Yet he persists in his quest. In this case, Camila is the victim of Pancho's inflexibility. Her life and her dreams are placed on hold while he pursues an impossible objective. More significantly, Camila loses her one chance to lead a normal life—by societal standards—when her relationship with Scott Andrews comes to an end because of her father's demands.

Closely related to Pancho's stubbornness is his immaturity. The patriarch of the Henríquez Ureña clan is self-centered to the extreme. His desires and his wishes always come before those of others, including the members of his family. In a leitmotif that appears throughout Pancho's characterization, the narrative equates him to a child. Hostos comments about how Salomé is obliged to act as a mother, with firmness, toward Pancho. In another instance, Salomé expresses her hope that Pancho will mature and begin to act as a good husband. Tivisita, his second wife, constitutes another victim of his self-centeredness: she dies exhausted "from being the wife of private-citizen Pancho" (207). His childish demands are thus portrayed as capable of sending others to their graves. Pancho's sons, realizing this, choose to move far away from their father, and they seldom visit him. Camila, on the other hand, suffers through many years because of her irascible father.

Although Salomé finds the physical part of her marriage satisfying, Pancho's emotional distance troubles her. At home he is so self-absorbed that he fails to take notice of the feelings of his wife and children. Everything in the Henríquez Ureña household revolves around him. Thus, Pancho is incapable of understanding the pain that his infidelity inflicts upon Salomé. Early in the narrative, Pancho's flirtation with other women foreshadows his subsequent actions. Pancho's affair in France, and later his attentions toward Tivisita while Salomé is ill, highlights his total separation from the feelings of others. Nevertheless, in spite of Pancho's grave shortcomings, the members of the Henríquez Ureña family still love him.

Francisco Henríquez, as the Dominican-American writer recreates him, is a man of extremes. It is as if Alvarez created two different characters in one. This is reflected in the several names she gives him: Pancho, Papancho and, in one instance, Sancho Pancho. They represent the charming, domineering, and at times simple sides of the character. Although Pancho's portrayal is not entirely sympathetic, he is endowed with traits that help to redeem him somewhat.

Pancho often displays a soft, loving side. This is evident in his love for animals, which also serves as a humorous device. He can also be sensitive. Pancho is a lover of poetry and art. Furthermore, he plays an important role in bringing Salomé out of her self-imposed isolation. He promotes her work—although he acts at times like a svengali charting her every career move. However, it is Pancho who introduces Salomé to the positivist model of thought. This, in the end, helps Salomé discover the roles that satisfy her the most: the roles of educator and of mother.

Pedro Henríquez Ureña, as stated in the beginning of this chapter, is the best known member of the family. As the narrative, told from Camila's perspective, reminds us: "[Pedro is] more famous than their mother ever was" (108). Endowed with a superb intelligence, in fiction as well as in reality, Pedro became well known through his writings and his research regarding Latin American literature. Pedro Henríquez Ureña was the first Hispanic to become Norton Lecturer at Harvard University since the Spanish-born philosopher and poet, Jorge Santayana (1863–1952). Pedro's books and essays on literature are still read and cited today, although nearly half a century has passed since his death.

Pedro is also recognized for his stand against Rafael Trujillo's dictatorship. Unlike his brother Max, Pedro refused to collaborate with the Dominican government. To accept a government post would have meant economic security for him. Trujillo would have handsomely rewarded the cooperation of the country's leading intellectual—not to mention the son of Salomé Ureña. However, because of his political convictions, Pedro turns down a comfortable life. Pedro's stance is a source of pride for Camila.

The price of Pedro's political integrity, however, is a life of exile. He can't return to his homeland. Living far from the "patria" takes a toll on him. When Camila sees him again after many years apart, he looks exhausted and worn. In Argentina, where Pedro married and settled, he has to teach at two or three universities to support his family. Ironically, in Camila's perspective, although Pedro refused Trujillo's money, he has sold out to materialism in order to give his wife and daughters a comparatively high standard of living. Camila criticizes Pedro because he no longer works for the love of literature, but rather to pay for the women in his life to have nice things.

One thing that Pedro and Camila have always been at odds over is his conservatism. In particular, he strongly condemns Camila's relationship with Marion. It all begins while they attend graduate school together. Pedro spies on her because he thinks that she is having a secret relationship with an American man. When Pedro discovers the truth he is horrified. He severely criticizes Camila for her perverted lifestyle. He warns the family against allowing Marion to visit Camila in Cuba. Pedro's strict sexual codes are satisfied when he learns of Camila's relationship with Domingo, the sculptor. Camila's heterosexuality makes him happy. His sister's happiness is secondary. What is important to Pedro is that she comport herself sexually in an orthodox manner.

In spite of their problems, the affection between Pedro and Camila is genuine. Both Salomé and Camila have a soft spot for Pedro in their hearts. Moreover, before dying, Salomé entrusts Camila to Pedro. This makes the bond between brother and sister unbreakable. In spite of time, distance, and personal differences, the siblings remain loving toward one another until the end.

Pedro, however, is perhaps the sibling that remains most devoted to his mother's memory. He considered his greatest achievement to be the son of Salomé Ureña. In the end, he wants to be remembered for his relationship to her. Pedro viewed her legacy as much more important than his own. That is why his final request was that he be buried alongside Salomé.

LITERARY DEVICE: METAPHOR

A metaphor is a figure of speech in which one thing is described in terms of another. Thus, a metaphor suggests a common quality that is shared by different things, ideas, or actions. Julia Alvarez, an accomplished poet as well as novelist, creates effective metaphors that link together various notions or characteristics of the world of poetry, poets, emotions, and politics.

In the metaphors that link poetry and poets, the reader encounters references to the nature of poetry, the importance of talent, the price a poet pays to exercise his or her craft, the comfort one can find in art, and the recognition awarded to the successful artist. Salomé's father, Nicolás Ureña, provides a metaphor that becomes an important leitmotif or recurring statement or image in the first part of the novel. Proud of his daughter's talent, Nicolás repeatedly claims that he plays the flute because he has given Salomé the trumpet. This metaphor suggests two things: first, his acknowledgement that her talent is superior to his and, second, that because of her talent she has little option in life but to write sonorous verses that awaken everyone. Later in the novel, after her father's death, Salomé enters into a deep depression that lasts for two years. Fittingly, the end of Salomé's doldrums is signaled by the sound of a street band playing during the feast of Corpus Christi. In particular, the sounds of the trumpet and the flute announce the awakening of the dormant muse.

Every artist pays a price to exercise his or her craft. Early in Salomé's life as a poet, Don Eloy hires her to write poems to help him seduce a woman. The payment she receives is a basket of guavas. However, the fruit is full of worms. This metaphor suggests that an artist must remain true to her or his art. Any deviation, any prostitution of an artist's talent will receive payment in kind. Shortchanging one's talent may not be worth the price, because every poet also pays an emotional toll for his or her creations. As Salomé's father often reminds her: "Tears are the ink of the poet." This metaphor indicates that pain is a part of the poet's creative process; that the best verses are the result of experiences that disturb its creator.

Writing poetry, nevertheless, can also be a source of comfort. When Salomé weighs the risks involved in committing to a relationship with Pancho, her mother urges her to take a chance. The woman understands perfectly that one must take risks for the sake of love, and she sees Pancho as Salomé's best chance for happiness. To Salomé's doubts, the mother responds with the metaphor that poetry will be the net that catches her should things go wrong. In other words, if the relationship with Pedro goes awry, Salomé can always turn to her creative endeavors for solace.

Towards the end of Salomé's life, she travels by boat to Puerto Plata. This, in essence, constitutes her final voyage. It recalls countless such journeys that are present throughout the pages of literature. These journeys are confined to the heroes of the story. To reinforce this metaphor, Alvarez designates Salomé a "queen" who, on her final trip, has the opportunity to bid farewell to her "grieving kingdom" (305). The metaphor, then, conveys Salomé's importance to her people. As the national poet, she reigns over the hearts of her fellow Dominicans, and they are in pain when they witness that her death is near.

In the Name of Salomé also includes metaphors that help the reader grasp the emotions and sentiments of the characters. Items found in a box—curls, wedding earrings, baby teeth, a broken Dominican flag, and others—serve as memory markers. The items constitute metaphors that bring to Camila's mind, as well as to the reader's, various incidents from the past that are emotional in nature. Other metaphors convey a character's dislike or nervousness toward a person or situation. For instance, Camila links the story of Hansel and Gretel to her feelings toward her stepmother, Tivisita. Appropriately, Camila acknowledges that the metaphor is far from adequate when she laments that Tivisita has been difficult to hate because she is kind, patient, and understanding. To reinforce this, Alvarez introduces the metaphor of Camila's stained birthday dress. Both Camila and her aunt Ramona believe that the dress is ruined forever when chocolate cake is spilled on it during a birthday party. However, Tivisita, as loving and patient as ever, works on the dress until it looks like new. The dress, then, becomes a metaphor that illustrates the stepmother's genuinely loving nature and accentuates Camila's guilt.

Love, both passionate and filial, is also described through metaphors in the novel. When Pancho awkwardly insinuates his love for Salomé during a tutoring session, it seems a chaste affair. However, to convey the underlying passion, Alvarez superimposes the declaration of love on a lesson about how flowers reproduce. Thus, in this gentle metaphor, the reader understands that the attraction goes beyond merely two people drawn to each other through poetry. Later, after Salomé's death, Pedro, or Pibín, employs a metaphor that helps the three-year-old Camila understand the importance of keeping their mother alive in their memories. He tells her that heaven is for the dead, and that they must keep Salomé forever in their hearts so that she may live on.

How Camila interprets her mother's poems in an attempt to answer life's questions constitutes the most significant metaphor with regard to the character's quest for meaning. Her efforts, though, are futile. Camila realizes this when she states that the game is getting out of hand. Camila's search for answers within her mother's verses is reinforced in the structure of In the Name of Salomé by Alvarez's decision to name each chapter after the title of one of Salomé's poems. In this manner, the mother's and daughter's journeys become one. They find meaning and love in each other.

The final metaphor to discuss is Camila's selection of her burial spot. Rodolfo, her half-brother, urges her to be buried alongside her mother. Camila refuses. She states that she could not stand the crowds who visit the national poet. Instead, Camila chooses to be interred with Rodolfo's family. She selects a corner on the bottom level of the three-tiered outdoor vault. Camila's nieces protest, stating that no one will see her there because she'll be too close to the ground, and the weeds would cover her headstone. But that is how Camila prefers it. She has come to terms with her place in this notable family. The selection of her final resting spot, then, becomes a metaphor for her acceptance of what her life has been. Camila, until Alvarez's novel, of course, is the least remembered member of the Henríquez Ureña family. However, that is fine with her. Therefore, through this metaphor we learn that Camila, at last, is truly at peace with her identity.

THEMATIC ISSUES

The predominant theme of In the Name of Salomé is the desire of the characters to live life as a work of art, particularly as works of literature. To a great degree, in Alvarez's novel, a character's stance toward literature determines the paths his or her existence will take. The importance of living one's life in a literary fashion is especially true for the members of the Henríquez Ureña clan. They, as do other minor characters, define themselves according to the place they occupy in the literary world.

Beginning with Nicolás Ureña, Salomé's father, the reader encounters a character whose life is steeped in literature. In addition to Nicolás's own identity as a poet, he plays a crucial role in forming the Dominican national poet. The written word informs his life, and he passes this trait on to his descendants. The narrative describes the room where his daughters visit him as full of books, old newspapers, quills, and ink. Nicolás writes to the rhythm of his words, and in between drinks he reads his verses to his daughters. His creativity inspires them. Thus, poetry becomes what binds Nicolás to his offspring.

Salomé chooses literature as her contribution to help free her country. Her choice is highly effective. Her works, in spite of being critical of Spanish rule, are published because the verses rhyme. The patriotic sentiments of her verses instantly guarantee her place in Dominican history. When the citizens of Santo Domingo, in an effort that Pancho leads, present Salomé with an award for her poetry, her life is changed forever. She earns greater recognition than any Dominican poet before her. But more importantly, she also gains a suitor in Pancho. In fact, it is her talent that draws him into her life.

Salomé's days as an artist, however, are numbered. After she marries she devotes her time and energy to endeavors other than poetry. In particular, Salomé becomes a wife, mother, and educator. Although she often hears the voice of the muse, she silences it in favor of her work for others. Salomé still writes poetry after her marriage, but the bulk of her oeuvre is complete by then.

Pancho attempts to lead an artistic existence as well. He writes verses. But they are of little merit. More of note is that he becomes Salomé's editor. As such, Pancho changes her verses to suit his taste rather than hers. Thus, Pancho's artistic identity is far from sterling. This is best illustrated after Ramona, Salomé's sister, discovers that Pancho and Tivisita have been corresponding while Salomé lays ill in bed. In a remarkable literary simile, the angry Ramona compares the future couple to another illicit couple—the Italian poet Dante Alighieri and his lifelong inspiration, Beatrice. However, in an act that helps somewhat to redeem Pancho, he dies after retrieving an anthology of Salomé's poems from the bookshelf. Thus, at the moment of his death, he turns to Salomé's literary personae for comfort and meaning.

Pedro, the eldest son, devotes his entire life to literature. Although he also writes poetry, he makes his greatest mark as a literary critic. In fact, through his scholarly activities, Pedro Henríquez Ureña becomes far better known throughout the Spanish-speaking world than his mother. His writings on Latin American literature constitute his legacy. Camila admires her big brother for his intelligence and insight. She shares her own poetry with him, and although his candid remarks bring her own poetic dreams to an end, she continues to love and respect him.

Camila, of course, is the character that most consciously attempts to recreate her mother's literary life. From birth she is locked into trying to live up to a remarkable artistic heritage. Camila is condemned to look back to her mother's literary legacy to try to find her own place in the world. Her name, Camila, is itself inspired by literature. It is taken from Florian's novel *Numa Pompilius*. During Camila's adolescence, while sitting alone at night amid the books of the family library, she wonders who she is meant to be. Because of her family's literary prominence, Camila grows up surrounded by other writers. Thus, she fervently wants to be part of this world. Relatively late in life, Camila tries her hand at writing poetry. Rather than being recognized as Salomé's daughter and Pedro's little sister, Camila wants to be accepted for her own talent. However, Camila abandons her dream of becoming a poet. Her only recourse is to find meaning in her mother's poetry. Happily, though, in her later years, she discovers that her place is to be the keeper of the family's legacy. Camila becomes the historian as well as the archivist of the Henríquez Ureña family. And it is in this role that she shares her family's story, as well as her own, with the reader.

Other renowned literary figures appear in the novel. In addition to the members of the Henríquez Ureña family, the reader encounters such Hispanic literary luminaries as the Dominicans José Castellanos and José Joaquín Pérez; the Spaniards Juan Ramón Jiménez, Pedro Salinas, and Jorge Guillén; the Puerto Rican Eugenio Hostos; and the Cuban José Martí. These eminent writers are well known to students of Hispanic literature. Their legacies still endure. Thus, it can be claimed that *In the Name of Salomé* constitutes a portrait of individuals who have lived their artistic vision to the fullest. For all of them, life and literature are undistinguishable from one another.

In the Name of Salomé, like each of Alvarez's previous novels, explores the theme of dictatorships. The panoramic account through decades of Dominican history allows the reader to learn about other lesser-known dictators, other than Rafael Trujillo. The reader encounters the surnames of Báez, Lilis, and Meriño. Throughout the generations of the Henríquez Ureña family, Dominican dictators have sought the support of its members. Lilis recites Salomé's poems to prove his patriotism. He provides Pancho with a scholarship to study in France. Decades later, Trujillo offers both Max and Pedro important posts in his cabinet. Both brothers accept, but shortly thereafter Pedro's political convictions force him to resign. Max, on the other hand, remains in Trujillo's cabinet, and as a consequence he is remembered as a collaborator of one of Latin America's most corrupt dictatorships. However, even the seemingly independent Camila is susceptible to Trujillo's influence. She receives a pension from the Dominican government. This keeps her, for some time, from speaking out against Trujillo. Furthermore, the stances the siblings take toward Trujillo's dictatorship prove divisive. In the end, both Pedro and Camila distance themselves from Max because of his loyalty to Trujillo.

U.S. intervention in Latin American politics is another theme the novel explores. U.S. foreign policy toward Latin America in the first half of the twentieth century directly affects the family. In fact, Pancho is forced out of the presidency as the result of the U.S. Marine invasion of the Dominican Republic. Other characters, in particular Martí and Hostos, were strong advocates of Panamericanism—a doctrine which touts equality and respect among all of the nations in the continent. However, the failure of this notion is perfectly illustrated in the manner in which Papancho loses his presidency. Because the family patriarch refuses to yield to U.S. political demands, he is forced to abdicate the highest office in his nation. Furthermore, as Pancho attempts to meet with President Harding to regain power, the White House ignores his requests. As a consequence, Pancho dies an embittered man. His only recourse in his quest for justice is to name the family pig after Teddy Roosevelt.

The final theme that deals with Latin American politics is the Cuban Revolution. This theme is central to Camila's character development. Camila, a Dominican exile residing in Cuba, becomes involved in protests against the dictatorship of Fulgencio Batista. Because of her opposition to Batista, she spends two weeks in prison. Immediately after her release, to insure her safety, Camila moves to the United States. The triumph of the Cuban Revolution, led by Fidel Castro, coincides with her retirement from Vassar. Uncertain about the future direction of her life, Camila decides to answer Castro's call for people who want to help build a new country. She believes that the country her mother had dreamed about can be built in Cuba. Eventually, because of the political tensions between the United States and the newly formed communist nation, Camila loses her retirement pension. But she doesn't mind. She finds it more important to place her experience as an educator at the service of the Revolution. It is here, where factory workers respond warmly to Salomé's poetry, that she finds meaning. Cuba, Camila asserts, is where illiteracy has been abolished, and where the true revolution of the imagination can take place. More importantly, it is where she comes to the realization that her life was not that different from her mother's. After all, above everything else, both women sacrificed their personal needs in order to educate those less privileged than themselves.

Another theme *In the Name of Salomé* explores is Camila's sexual orientation. Throughout the first half of the novel there are elements that foreshadow this theme. These include a reference to Marion and Camila having lived through so much together that it is best buried in the past. There is also a reference to their "commitment" to one another (36). Since the theme is not addressed overtly as the plot develops, the reader begins to put the pieces of this puzzle together little by little. Because of temporal and cultural mores, Camila is forced into a difficult decision between family and Marion, society and love. Camila chooses to lead a seemingly conventional life in order to avoid scandalizing society. To a great extent, it is Pedro's spying and his condemnation of Camila's "perverted" lifestyle that forces her to reject a life with Marion. On the other hand, Camila is also disturbed by Marion's domineering ways. A third factor is that society, especially Hispanic society, had not come to terms—and many argue has yet to come to terms—with same-sex relationships. Thus, Camila is obliged to place her needs on hold again in order to live a life that is acceptable to others. She represses the attraction she has experienced since adolescence for other women. Like many individuals in the same situation, Camila has to deny her sexual identity so as to not to offend others.

Another theme, positivism, is introduced through Eugenio Hostos. Positivism is a philosophical theory of knowledge associated with the nineteenth-century French philosopher Auguste Comte. Positivism holds that the observable, or "positive," data of sense experience constitutes the sole basis for assertions about matters of fact. Only the truths of logic and mathematics are additionally admitted. Thus, the speculative claims of theology and metaphysics, regarded as the primitive antecedents of "positive" or scientific thoughts, are discarded. Comte foreshadows a progression in the mental development of humankind. In the French philosopher's construct, men and women would evolve into beings that choose reason over superstition, and negotiation over violence. Positivism would have a significant impact in Latin American politics and educational practices. Individuals like Pancho and Salomé, who hope for a nation of thinking, caring citizens, see in positivism a way to achieve this objective. This is why Eugenio Hostos, the Puerto Rican essayist and positivist, is such a strong presence in the novel. However, more conservative elements of society, particularly the military and the Catholic Church, find positivism dangerous to traditions well established over the centuries. Ultimately, the reader sees the positivist model for education defeated. When Camila returns to visit the school Salomé founded, she finds no evidence of her mother's positivist educational model. However,

Camila does note that, in her opinion, the society that has come closest to achieving the positivist dream has been Cuba.

In the Name of Salomé also delves into the theme of *la patria*. In fact, a verse from one of Salomé's poems appears prior to the beginning of the narrative. It asks *¿Qué es la patria?* (What is a homeland?). *Patria*, a Spanish word, defies translation. The English-language terms "homeland," "motherland," or the more commonly used "country," lack the emotional resonance that *patria* conveys in Spanish. For Spanish-speakers, the word *patria* can bring tears to their eyes. The word encompasses all that is good, all that is loved unconditionally, and all one would sacrifice for one's birthplace. *Patria* comes from the same Latin root that in English gives us the word "patriotism." When the characters of *In the Name of Salomé* use the word *patria*, they are also attempting to define it. This is because throughout Latin America's history the group that controls the definition of *patria* is the one that governs the country. In light of the endless struggle of the Dominican Republic—and of other Latin American nations—to establish a just and equitable society, the leitmotif of *la patria* acquires a sense of urgency. Hence the significance of Salomé's poetic query, "*¿Qué es la patria?*"

The theme of racial and ethnic discrimination has been prominent in Alvarez's novels. *In the Name of Salomé* is no exception. The narrative begins with a description of Camila's racial identity. Her ethnicity constitutes a central feature in the character's quest for a sense of self. Africa is present in the ancestry of the Henríquez Ureña family. Part of Salomé's own insecurities can be traced to this heritage. Her African features are the cause of some anguish in the poet's youth. In adulthood, though, Salomé learns to live comfortably with her ancestry. In death, however, Pancho orders a portrait of Salomé that erases all traces of her African heritage. The denial of Salomé's blackness becomes a metaphor for Camila's futile attempt to emulate her mother. Through Pancho's manipulation, a fantasy of Salomé has been created. The fantasy covers Salomé's personal, artistic, and ethnic identity. Thus Camila can never live up to the ideal Pancho created. Ironically, Pancho also has been subject to discrimination because of his Jewish heritage. However, since members of his family behave like "good Christians," the Henríquez Ureñas are tolerated in spite of their religious identity.

In the United States, the Henríquez Ureña siblings experience racism because of their skin color. Members of the Ku Klux Klan burn a wooden cross in front of Marion's North Dakota home when Camila visits. Camila witnesses how black jazz musicians who entertain white customers are forced to enter and exit through the rear of the club. The narrative also reveals how Max, an accomplished jazz pianist, endured the same humiliating circumstances when he played in a band. Furthermore, immediately after the siblings tour Lincoln's monument in Washington D.C., they are refused entry into a coffee shop because of their dark complexion. Thus, in this stark superimposition, the ideals that Lincoln represents in the American psyche are betrayed.

A final theme to discuss is also one that appears frequently in Alvarez's novels: cultural displacement. This theme revolves around Pedro and Camila. Because they are part black as well as foreigners, they experience both disorientation and discrimination in the United States. As graduate students in a xenophobic World War I America, Pedro and Camila are often stopped and questioned regarding their ethnicity. The Boy Spies of America and a group of war protesters stop them for simply looking different than most "Americans." A local newspaper writes an article about them that significantly deviates from the truth. Brother and sisters are portrayed as strong supporters of U.S. foreign policy when in fact they have been victims of it. However, the press assumes the right to publish what is good for national pride rather than the truth. Because of these incidents, Pedro refuses to remain in the United States after completing his doctoral studies. The racial and ethnic discrimination he has experienced there affects him deeply, and he rejects what could have been a comfortable, distinguished career teaching in a U.S. university. Camila, on the other hand, chooses to remain in the States. However, she too suffers from indignities. These range from people not taking the time to properly learn how to pronounce her name, to the knowledge that Latino lives are disposable for Americans. People in her adopted homeland, she thinks, don't interest themselves in the heroes and heroines of minor countries until a movie is made about them. Consequently, when Camila retires, she leaves the United States without hesitation. Her emotional investment in this country has been minimal because she was never fully accepted as an "American."

A FEMINIST READING OF *IN THE NAME OF SALOMÉ*

As mentioned in Chapter 3, one of the trademarks of feminist criticism is its diversity. Nevertheless, the common purpose of all feminist criticism can be identified as the exposition of the mechanisms upon which patriarchal society rests and continues to sustain itself. Thus, the ultimate objective of feminist inquiry is fundamentally a "political" one, since it seeks to transform social relations. Keeping these concerns in mind, we will examine *In the Name of Salomé* from a feminist perspective.

An important feature for many feminist critics is to draw attention to women writers who create in the historically male-dominated world of literature. As the novel's title suggests, the story revolves around the life of a woman. In fact, early in the narrative the reader discovers that Alvarez actually explores the lives of two women. Moreover, upon closer examination, the title can be considered subversive, even heretical. It challenges the male-dominated universe in which the women dwell. In Catholicism, prayers are initiated with the Sign of the Cross that includes the phrase: "In the name of the Father and of the Son and of the Holy Spirit." Ramona, Salomé's sister, teaches Camila to include her mother as the latter figure of the Trinity so that Salomé's memory will always remain alive in the daughter. The inclusion of ". . . and of my mother, Salomé," constitutes a transgression of traditional Catholic beliefs and hierarchical practices. This transgression offends and frightens Papancho. He demands the return of his children, who have been in Ramona's care, after he learns that the aunt had taught his daughter the adulterated version of the Sign of the Cross. However, in spite of the cautionary measures, the father cannot erase the transformed phrase from Camila's mind. She carries it with her into old age, uttering it whenever she feels in need of Salomé's blessing. Thus, when the reader looks at the title closely, one can assume that the patriarchal order of the universe will be challenged throughout the narrative.

Indeed, a major challenge for the women characters is to exercise their creative autonomy in a male-dominated culture that operates under the highly restrictive codes of machismo. In a macho, hyper-patriarchal society, a man has the unconditional power and authority to make decisions for the women under his protectorate. Furthermore, in a male-centered culture, men attempt to control women's behavior. Moreover, in a society characterized by machismo, women's voices have largely been silenced; their stories have received little or no attention. That is why *In the Name of Salomé* will resonate so strongly among Latinas and other women: it is the story of a renown Dominican poet and her daughter who speak on behalf of an entire population that historically has been without voice. That Julia Alvarez tells their story at all constitutes a significant victory for Latinas.

Women in a patriarchal society are for the most part powerless. For instance, throughout the narrative, the men who are most important to

Salomé and Camila attempt to control them. After Salomé's marriage, Pancho dictates most of her decisions. In fact, while Pancho is studying in France, his brother, Federico, acts as his proxy. He spies on her, assuming the place of the husband in Pancho's absence. Camila also suffers because the men in her family control her life. Papancho thoroughly dominates her. She is subject to obeying all his whims. Camila cannot seem to escape Papancho's control. During the brief period that Camila is away from him while attending graduate school, Pedro, her brother, acts as Papancho's proxy. He spies on her as Federico spied on his mother. Later, after Papancho's death, Camila becomes involved in protests against Batista's dictatorship in Cuba. In this instance, Max attempts to control Camila's life. He tries to curtail her political activism.

Men, on the other hand, are free to engage in whatever behaviors or activities they wish. This includes the right to have extramarital affairs. Salomé's mother suffered her husband's infidelities. In fact, it was the reason she left Nicolás. Salomé also suffered because of Pancho's unfaithfulness. Later, when Salomé is ill, she witnesses how her husband develops a relationship with Tivisita. As her death approaches, the reader has the certainty that she is acutely aware that Pancho will choose Tivisita to take her place.

Pancho's infidelity also affects Camila. Because of the manner in which her father and Tivisita came together, Camila can never trust her stepmother. In addition, Camila lives her entire life with the open wound of her "Paris family." She realizes that she has a half-sister with whom she will never develop a relationship. Camila has vague news of her other family, and because of the circumstances surrounding their existence, the gap between them cannot be bridged. Camila never fills this void in her life because she needs to remain loyal to her mother, to respect her pain.

A feature of a society that subscribes to machismo is that there are double-standards. Men are allowed to pursue the sexual conquest of women. In fact, in this enterprise, "their brio [is] applauded" (93). Women, on the other hand, must seek companionship with great discretion. They must not give evidence of their desire for a man. Thus, men feel entitled to a full sexual life, regardless of who it may affect; while women must always be chaste and demure. Don Eloy, who hires Salomé to write poems for him so that he may seduce a woman, exemplifies the double standard. He blatantly states that men are free to pursue sexual satisfaction outside of their marriages (54–55). Pancho believes that because he is away from home during his medical studies he also has the right, as a man, to find companionship. Furthermore, the primary reason he has his brother spy on Salomé is to insure that she remain faithful. Moreover, when Pancho returns from France he is bewildered because Salomé initially denies him his rightful place in bed. Thus, the double standards in patriarchal society represent absolute sexual freedom for men and sexual repression for women.

In order for women to accept their limitations in such a society, they are trained from childhood to accept the roles that tradition has established for them. During Salomé's childhood, girls are taught the alphabet, how to sit, stand, pour water, pray the Rosary, and say the Stations of the Cross. In addition, they can learn how to knit, sew, crochet, read, but not how to write. This constitutes a limited education, one that restricts a woman's choices in adulthood to being a wife and mother. However, although patriarchal society imposes these restrictions, most women subscribe to them. It is considered scandalous to deviate from the norm, to seek an education equal to what a man is entitled. Furthermore, in a patriarchy women are taught to be passive. Salomé's courtship with Pancho reflects this. She yearns to reach out to touch him, but doesn't do so because it is considered inappropriate for a woman to be the aggressor in a relationship.

In a macho society, women are obliged to keep their sexual needs within the confines of marriage. First of all, a woman's honor is equated to her status as a virgin. That is why Pedro spies on his sister: to insure her virtue and protect her prospects for marriage. Protecting a woman's honor is also why Federico spies on Salomé. Furthermore, a woman's sexual expression is to be kept secret from everyone, including herself. Women are expected to remain ignorant of all sexual matters. Masturbation, for example, is portrayed as a perversion brought on by a woman's excessive knowledge about sex (57–58). For Camila, living a full sexual life is a particularly difficult task, since her attraction to other women is considered aberrant in patriarchal society. Because of her lesbianism, she is denied the freedom to love another person fully. Camila, then, is eventually forced to choose a life of celibacy in order to please family and society. Once again the reader encounters a woman who has to place her own needs in abeyance in order to please others.

Because of the passivity ingrained in women in patriarchal culture, they are trained to place their needs and desires on hold. The needs of their husband, their family, and society come first. Salomé makes an immense personal sacrifice when she forsakes her poetic voice in order to care for her family and to direct a school for girls. Raising her three boys and her work as a teacher consume her life. In quiet moments the muse tries to return, but Salomé tells it to hush. Another character, Tivisita, dies because the task of "being the wife of private-citizen Pancho" exhausted her (207). Tivisita's devotion to her husband, combined with his excessive demands, drives her to an early grave. Camila's life is devoted to family as well; in particular to meeting her father's demands after Tivisita's death. Because of this, Camila relegates her personal needs to the background. Patriarchal society has taught these women to sacrifice their hopes, dreams, and aspirations for the sake of the men in their lives.

The most pernicious control men have over women appears, at least on the surface, to be an abstract one. In the novel, men exercise considerable control over the creative expressions of women. During the literary gatherings that Salomé attends, women are not allowed to give their opinions except when called upon. When Salomé publishes a love poem for the first time, the sensibilities of patriarchal society prompt several women to demand that the award the literary society had earlier presented to her be stripped away. Later, after Salomé's marriage, Pancho assumes the task of editing her first book of poetry. In the process, he takes control of Salomé's words, changing her poetry to suit his poetic notions. When Salomé writes a personal poem, "Vespertina," Pancho promptly dismisses it. He tells her not to write in a minor key, and orders her to write poems only to *la patria*. Pancho's dismissal angers Salomé, who feels that she is just beginning to discover her voice as a woman. Toward the end of Salomé's life, however, Pancho acknowledges his manipulation of Salomé's poetic voice. After he asks her to write a poem to commemorate the 400th anniversary of Columbus's first voyage to the Americas, he apologizes for having halted her development as a poet. Pancho, though, is not the only man in Salomé's life to reject the poems considered personal. In death, her son Pedro rejects her sentimental verses. He excludes them from the anthology of her work that he edited. And in life, Eugenio Hostos, whom she much admires because of his positivist beliefs, rejects her poetic endeavors in their totality.

Men who are important to Camila reject her written work as well. While studying for her masters, Camila's academic advisor rejects her proposal to write a thesis on the writings of Eugenio Hostos. The professor favors something more "classical," less tied to her personal life. Later, it is Camila's beloved brother, Pedro, who stunts her growth as a poet. His rejection of her personal poems devastates her. After Pedro's forthright criticism of her creative work, Camila ceases to write. Thus men control the voices of women in the novel.

In the Name of Salomé, however, contains a few models of men who at times reject patriarchal codes of behavior. Indeed, these characters foreshadow the advent of men who are against sexism. Nicolás, Salomé and Ramona's father, insists that his daughters receive a better education than women at the time are allowed. Because of his insistence, their education, in every respect, is equal to a man's. The Dominican intellectual, Don Eliseo Grullón, plays a pivotal role in Salomé's life. He is the first character to express his admiration for her poetry. Furthermore, according to Salomé, he is the first man she has met who treats women as more than objects. While Pancho is oblivious to women's issues, his mentor, Eugenio Hostos, is an early feminist. Although Hostos rejects Salomé's poetry, for he considers writing poetry an activity unworthy of a positivist, he clearly understands women's issues. In fact, Salomé is envious of his wife. She wishes that Pancho were as enlightened as Hostos regarding a woman's needs and rights. Thus, from the perspective of a reader who closely examines gender issues, the narrative is balanced. Men are portrayed fairly. While most subscribe to the codes of patriarchal society, a few exhibit an understanding of how unfair societal restrictions are to women.

Mostly, though, it is up to women to struggle so that their conditions can be improved. Salomé's mother, Gregoria, leaves her husband in spite of how difficult it will be for her to become independent. Her determination, nevertheless, is rewarded. She and her sister purchase a house together—something unheard of at the time. In this manner, Salomé grows up among strong, independent women who believe that a woman needs to become well-educated and self-reliant.

Salomé will later use her education to record in verse the unfair conditions women face. Salomé writes a poem in protest when she learns about a pregnant teenager who is abandoned by her lover. Upon publication, this poem causes a furor. The poem and its theme brings to mind the first great feminist of the Americas, the seventeenth-century Mexican poet, Sor Juana Inés de la Cruz. Because of Salomé's conviction that the lives of women need improvement, she opens the first school for girls on the island. Ironically, among the women she teaches to read and write is Tivisita, who will later use this skill to exchange letters with Pancho. Regardless of this incident, Salomé understands how important it is to help women become independent.

Another example of a strong woman is Marion. She is loud, irreverent, aggressive, and strong. Marion exhibits little respect for patriarchal conventions (81–83). A dance teacher, Marion's performances foreshadow

the Feminist Movement, and as a consequence they are highly controversial. Because Marion's activism on behalf of women's causes creates
problems for her, Marion retires early from teaching. She reaches an
agreement with her future husband, and they marry primarily to keep
each other company. Paradoxically, married to a man of economic
means, she gains the independence and freedom to do as she wishes.

Camila, on the other hand, is portrayed as insecure and passive. She
submits to the dictates of her family. In particular, Camila obeys her
demanding father. After Papancho's death, she begins her long journey
towards independence and self-confidence. First, however, Camila has
to free herself from the imposing figures of the Henríquez Ureña family.
Her mother's shadow hovers dauntingly above her. Ironically, then, it is
another's woman's legacy that weighs the most upon Camila. The key
moment of her independence arrives when an angry Dominican student
confronts Camila prior to a lecture commemorating the 100th anniversary of her mother's birth. Camila frees herself from reading a sterile
essay she had prepared for the occasion. Instead, prompted by the student's anger, Camila improvises a speech condemning Rafael Trujillo's
dictatorship. This is the true beginning of her journey to selfhood. There
still remains, however, a long road to travel. It is not until Camila gives
herself totally to the Cuban Revolution that she finds her place in the
world. The Epilogue of *In the Name of Salomé* portrays a leading character
that is in control of her life. Remarkably, in spite of the hardships Camila
faced as a woman, the reader cannot find a trace of bitterness in her. She
has made peace with her life and with her mother's legacy. Camila is
proud that of all the Henríquez Ureñas, she is the most whole, the most
complete, and the most happy.

That the stories of Salomé and Camila are told at all constitutes Julia
Alvarez's tribute to Dominican women. As *In the Time of the Butterflies*
and *In the Name of Salomé* attest, the island's history is full of tales of
brave women that merit telling. Therefore, Alvarez's dedication at the
beginning of the novel, "Quisqueyanas Valientes—This book is for you,"
acquires a greater significance when examined through a feminist lens.
Quisqueya is the indigenous name of the island prior to Columbus's arrival. Hence the epithet for Dominicans is *Quisqueyano* for a man, and
Quisqueyana for a woman. As Alvarez repeatedly reminds her readers
throughout her novels, many Dominican women have made enormous
sacrifices for their homeland. However, *Quisqueyanas* are still struggling
to be heard. Thus, through Alvarez's writings they have gained a measure of victory. Thanks to Alvarez's talents, tens of thousands of Amer-

ican readers are now able to penetrate what once was a closed world. The voices that have lingered in silence—the voices of the Mirabal sisters, and the voices of Salomé and Camila—now reverberate thanks to Julia Alvarez's vibrant, sparkling prose. And through the efforts of this Dominican-American writer, the victory of *Quisqueyanas* becomes a victory for women everywhere.

Bibliography

Note: Plume has released all of Alvarez's novels in paperback. The page numbers of the paperback and the hardcover editions published by Algonquin Books are the same.

WORKS BY JULIA ALVAREZ

Novels

How the García Girls Lost Their Accents. Chapel Hill: Algonquin Books, 1991.
In the Name of Salomé. Chapel Hill: Algonquin Books, 2000.
In the Time of the Butterflies. Chapel Hill: Algonquin Books, 1994.
¡Yo!. Chapel Hill: Algonquin Books, 1997.

Poetry

The Other Side/El Otro Lado. New York: Dutton, 1995.
Homecoming. New York: Plume, 1995.

Essays

Something to Declare. Chapel Hill: Algonquin Books, 1998.

Children's Books

The Secret Footprints. New York: Knopf, 2000.

Young Adult Books

How Tía Lola Came to Stay. New York: Knopf, 2001.

Cookbooks

The New Family Cookbook: Recipes for Nourishing Yourself and Those You Love (co-authored with Bill Eichner). White River Junction, VT: Chelsea Green Publishing, 2000.

Reviews and Essays by Julia Alvarez

"Alvarez Describes Home," a chapter on descriptive writing in *Writer's Choice: Composition and Grammar Text For Eighth Graders.* Glencoe: MacMillan/McGraw Hill, 1993.

"An American Childhood in the Dominican Republic." *The American Scholar,* Winter 1987.

"Black Behind the Ears." *Essence Magazine,* February 1993.

"Flight Plans." *The Washington Post Magazine,* August 13, 1995.

"Hold the Mayonnaise." *Hers* Column, *New York Times Magazine,* January 12, 1992; reprinted in *The McGraw Hill Reader.* New York: McGraw Hill Publishing Company, 1994; in *Aims and Options: A Themaic Approach to Writing.* Boston: Houghton Mifflin Company, 1994.

Introduction to Clarice Lispector's "The Smallest Woman in the World" in *You've Got to Read This: Contemporary American Writers Introduce Stories That Held Them in Awe.* New York: HarperPerennial, 1994.

"Learning English, My New Found Land." *New York Newsday,* February 22, 1993.

"My English." *Brújula/Compass,* Fall 1992.

"My Second Opera." *The Lane Series,* 1992–1993.

"Names/Nombres." *Nuestro,* March 1985; reprinted in *Beyond Expectations: Treasury of Literature.* New York: Harcourt, Brace Jovanovich, 1993; in *Shades of Gold: Treasury of Literature.* New York: Harcourt Brace and Company, 1995; in *Perspectives: Authentic Voices of Latinos.* North Billerica: Curriculum Associates, 1995.

"On Finding a Latino Voice." *The Washington Post Book World,* May 14, 1995.

"On 'One Art' by Elizabeth Bishop." *Touchstones: American Poets on a Favorite Poem.* Hanover: University Press of New England, ND.

"Quake Revives Nuclear Fears." *Burlington Free Press,* October 16, 1983.

"Silver Linings." *New Mexico Humanities Review,* Winter 1984.

"Translating a Look." *Allure Magazine,* March 1995.

"Voices: A Look Back at Dominican Humor." *Nuestro,* November 1984.

WORKS ABOUT JULIA ALVAREZ

General

Bing, Jonathan. "Julia Alvarez: Books That Cross Borders." *Publishers Weekly*, 16 December 1996: 38–39.

Fernandez, María Elena. "Two Sides of an American Identity." *Los Angeles Times*, March 23, 2000: E1 and E4.

Fichtner, Margarita. "Historical Fiction is Tricky, Julia Alvarez Admits." *Miami Herald*, June 28, 2000.

García-Tabor, María and Sirias, Silvio. "The Truth According to Your Characters: An Interview with Julia Alvarez." *Prairie Schooner*, Volume 74, Number 2, Summer 2000: 151–56.

Garza, Melita Marie. "Sharing Secrets." *Chicago Tribune*. November 21, 1994, 1 and 5.

"Julia Alvarez: Dominican-American Novelist and Poet." *Latino Biographies*. Paramus: Globe Fearon, 1994.

Lyons, Bonnie and Oliver, Bill. "Julia Alvarez: A Clean Windshield." *Passion and Craft: Conversations with Notable Writers*. Chicago: University of Illinois Press, 1998: 128–44.

Mena, Jennifer. "Women on the Verge." *Hispanic*, March 1995: 22–26.

O'Neill, Molly. "The Farm Team." *New York Times Magazine*, March 23, 1997: 67–68.

Prescott, Stephanie. "Julia Alvarez: Dominican Republic Storyteller." *Faces*, February 1999: 30–33.

Rosario-Sievert, Heather. "Conversation with Julia Alvarez." *Review: Latin American Literature and Art*. Spring 1997: 31–37.

REVIEWS AND CRITICISM

How the García Girls Lost Their Accents

Hoffman, Joan M. "She Wants to be Called Yolanda Now: Identity, Language, and the Third Sister in *How the García Girls Lost Their Accents*." *Bilingual Review*, January–April 1998: 21–28.

Mayock, Ellen C. "The Bicultural Construction of Self in Cisneros, Alvarez, and Santiago." *Bilingual Review*, September–December 1998: 223–30.

Miller, S. "Caught Between Two Cultures." *Newsweek*, April 20, 1992: 78–80.

Rifkind, D. "Speaking American." *New York Times Book Review*, October 6, 1991: 14.

Stavans, Ilan. "Daughters of Invention." *Commonweal*, April 10, 1992: 23–26.

Reviews of How the García Girls Lost Their Accents

Faces, February 1999: 46.
Hispanic Times Magazine, December 1991/January 1992: 24.
Library Journal, May 1, 1991: 102.
Publishers Weekly, April 5, 1991: 133.
Publishers Weekly, May 11, 1992: 69.
School Library Journal, September 1991: 292.
World Literature Today, Summer 1992: 516.

In the Time of the Butterflies

Birnbaum, Robert. "A Conversation with Julia Alvarez." *Stuff Magazine*, December 1994: 33–37.
"Butterfly Martyrs." *Islands*, January/February 1995.
Echevarría, Roberto González. "Sisters in Death." *New York Times Book Reviews*, December 18, 1994: 28.
Martínez, Elizabeth. "Of Passion and Politics." *Progressive*, July 1995: 39–43.
Miller, Susan. "Family Spats, Urgent Prayers." *Newsweek*, October 17, 1994: 77.
Morales, Ed. "Madam Butterfly." *Village Voice*, November 8, 1994: 13.
Mujica, Barbara. "The Sisters Mirabal." *World and I*, April 1995: 328–32.
———."On Politics and Literature." *Americas*, March/April 1995: 60.
Puleo, Gus. "Remembering and Reconstructing the Mirabal Sisters in Julia Alvarez's *In the Time of the Butterflies*." *Bilingual Review*, January–April 1998: 11–21.
Roth, Ava. "Sisters in Revolution." *Ms.*, September/October 1994: 79–81.
Stavans, Ilan. "Las Mariposas." *Nation*, November 7 1994: 552–56.
"Viva Latinas." *Harper's Bazaar*, September 1994: 222.

Reviews of In the Time of the Butterflies

Booklist, July 1994: 1892.
Glamour, October 1994: 176.
Hispanic, December 1994: 82.
Library Journal, August 1994: 123.
People, January 1, 1995: 26–27.
Publisher's Weekly, July 11, 1994: 62.
World Literature Today, Autumn 1995: 789.

Something to Declare

Brown, Rosellen. "Passing Through Customs." *Women's Review of Books*, November 1998: 7–9.

Nordin, Kendra. "A Writer's Journey to a New Land and a New Language." *Christian Science Monitor*, October 29, 1998: B7.

Reviews of Something to Declare

Booklist, August 1998: 1952.
Hispanic, March 1999: 72–74.
Library Journal, August 1998: 88.
Publisher's Weekly, July 13, 1998: 67.
School Library Journal, April 1999: 162.

¡Yo!

Frucht, Abby. "That García Girl." *New York Times Book Review*, 9 February 1997: 19.
Schneider, Bethany. "Hail to the Thief." *Elle*, January 1997: 44.

Reviews of ¡Yo!

Atlantic Monthly, February 1997: 110.
Booklist, September 15, 1996: 180.
Hispanic, March 1997: 68–70.
Library Journal, October 1, 1996: 124.
Ms., March/April 1997: 82.
People, January 20, 1997: 33.
Publishers Weekly, October 14, 1996: 62.
World Literature Today, Autumn 1997: 785.

In the Name of Salomé

Grossman, Judith. "*La Musa de la Patria*." *Women's Review of Books*, September 2000: 12–17.
"In the Name of *Quisqueya*." *Hispanic*, June 2000: 76–77.
Minzesheimer, Bob. "Salomé Dances Lyrically." *USA Today*, July 6, 2000: 6D.
Nordin, Kendra. "Recalling the Dreams of a Caribbean Past." *Christian Science Monitior*, July 6, 2000: 19.
Ruta, Suzanne. "Daughters of Revolution." *New York Times Book Review*, July 16, 2000: 24.
Wheeler, Kate. "Castro Converter." *Mirabella*, June/July 2000: 29–30.

Reviews of In the Name of Salomé

Entertainment Weekly, June 23 2000: 94.
Library Journal, May 1, 2000: 151.

Miami Herald, June 7, 2000.
Orlando Sentinel, August 9, 2000.

SECONDARY SOURCES

Turner, Victor. *Dramas, Fields, and Metaphors: Symbolic Action in Human Society.* Ithaca: Cornell University Press, 1974.

————. *The Ritual Process: Structure and Anti-Structure.* Chicago: Aldine, 1969.

van Gennep, Arnold. *Les Rites du Passage.* 1908. *The Rites of Passage.* Trans. Monika B. Vizedom and Gabrielle L. Caffee. London: Routledge and Kegan Paul, 1960.

Index

About the Author

SILVIO SIRIAS is Associate Professor of Spanish and U.S. Latino Literature at Ave Maria College of the Americas in San Marcos, Nicaragua. He has written scholarly articles on Alvarez and other Hispanic poets. Sirias is the editor of Salomon de la Selva's *Tropical Town and Other Poems*. He also co-edited, with Bruce Dick, *Conversations with Rudolfo Anaya*.

Critical Companions to Popular Contemporary Writers
First Series—*also available on CD-ROM*

V. C. Andrews
  by E. D. Huntley

Tom Clancy
  by Helen S. Garson

Mary Higgins Clark
  by Linda C. Pelzer

Arthur C. Clarke
  by Robin Anne Reid

James Clavell
  by Gina Macdonald

Pat Conroy
  by Landon C. Burns

Robin Cook
  by Lorena Laura Stookey

Michael Crichton
  by Elizabeth A. Trembley

Howard Fast
  by Andrew Macdonald

Ken Follett
  by Richard C. Turner

John Grisham
  by Mary Beth Pringle

James Herriot
  by Michael J. Rossi

Tony Hillerman
  by John M. Reilly

John Jakes
  by Mary Ellen Jones

Stephen King
  by Sharon A. Russell

Dean Koontz
  by Joan G. Kotker

Robert Ludlum
  by Gina Macdonald

Anne McCaffrey
  by Robin Roberts

Colleen McCullough
  by Mary Jean DeMarr

James A. Michener
  by Marilyn S. Severson

Anne Rice
  by Jennifer Smith

Tom Robbins
  by Catherine E. Hoyser and Lorena Laura Stookey

John Saul
  by Paul Bail

Erich Segal
  by Linda C. Pelzer

Gore Vidal
  by Susan Baker and Curtis S. Gibson